THE ANXIOUS INVESTOR

ALSO BY SCOTT NATIONS

A History of the United States in Five Crashes:
Stock Market Meltdowns That Defined a Nation

THE ANXIOUS INVESTOR

MASTERING

THE MENTAL GAME

OF INVESTING

SCOTT NATIONS

WM

WILLIAM MORROW
An Imprint of HarperCollins*Publishers*

FOR WENDI

This book is not designed to be a definitive investment guide or to take the place of advice from a qualified financial planner or other professional. Given the risk involved in investing of almost any kind, there is no guarantee that the investment methods suggested in this book will be profitable. The publisher and the author disclaim liability for any losses that may be sustained as a result of applying the methods suggested in this book.

FIRST EDITION

Designed by Elina Cohen
Growth line art courtesy of Shutterstock / Uthai pr
Charts and bar graphs courtesy of author

Library of Congress Cataloging-in-Publication Data has been applied for.

ISBN 978-0-06-306760-8

22 23 24 25 26 LSC 10 9 8 7 6 5 4 3 2 1

CONTENTS

THE ANXIOUS INVESTOR

Satan was rising from the earth. With pitchfork in hand, he was coming to claim more souls and one soul in particular was almost in his grasp. Above him an empty coffin dangled from the ceiling by a rope and the deadweight pulled the rope taut. On the side of the coffin was stenciled the name of its soon-to-be and intended occupant, Satan's quarry, Adolf Hitler. This hokey battle for Hitler's immortal soul wasn't being waged in Berlin or Bavaria but on the first floor of a department store in Iowa.

The Younkers Brothers department store was several times bigger than the next largest in the state. It occupied an entire block in downtown Des Moines where it sold men's, women's, and children's clothing, as well as furniture, furnishings, and personal items. It was suitably progressive for the capital's flagship department store; Younkers had installed air conditioning in 1934 and the state's first escalator—what locals called the "electric stairs"—in 1939, the same year Hitler started the war in Europe.

Everything changed at Younkers when the United States entered that war two years later. Rationing and shortages meant fewer items on its shelves. Nonetheless, the store urged Iowans to do their wartime duty and reminded them that they could fulfill that duty every time they visited. They were invited to the store's Liberty Hall to see a map, billed as the largest in Iowa, which charted the course of the war on all its fronts. They could listen to educational speeches and buy something for servicemen stationed abroad; Younkers helpfully offered a list of "Suggested Gifts for Soldiers" which included wristwatches, fountain pens, stationery, and smoking accessories. And shoppers could buy war bonds there too.

World War II cost the United States $296 billion—about $4 trillion in today's dollars—and more than half of that total came from investments that ordinary Americans made during seven war bond drives staged between 1941 and 1945. Younkers, as one of the central businesses in Iowa's largest city, became a hub for war bond sales. Employees sold bonds alongside those wristwatches and fountain pens, and 97 percent of all Younkers employees invested in bonds themselves through payroll deduction plans. Younkers sold at least $500,000 worth during each of the drives when the sales to customers and employees were combined. One of the store's cobblers, a Greek immigrant with a brother in the US Navy, sold $209,675 worth single-handedly.

Every American business selling war bonds got marketing help from the US government. Walnut Street outside the Younkers front door was filled with a display of captured German weapons during one drive. Shoppers who bought bonds could take a ride on one of two US Army tanks parked outside the store during the next. Signs nearby urged buyers to "label a bomb to your favorite enemy"—Germany or Japan, your choice—and a bond-buying mother could send the bomb her money helped build to Yamamoto, with delivery to be made by air. And during the third war bond drive, which urged Americans to "Back the Attack," as each sale got Younkers closer to its goal, window dressing riggers lowered Hitler's coffin a bit closer to that grasping papier-mâché Satan who stood next to a sign imploring shoppers to "Help Us Bury Hitler." Only in a global war, with passions and emotions unleashed, could Satan be made an ally by those working to sell an investment product.

The Younkers department store, and the US Treasury, had stumbled upon a fundamental truth of investing. They sold war bonds by appealing to investors' emotions rather than pitching them as worthwhile financial investments. Why? Because despite all of our modernity, learning, and market-focused technology, passions and emotions remain the most important aspect of investing. Learning about, understanding, and accounting for your own behavioral quirks can do more to improve your long-term investing results than even a roaring bull market can. Investors can also do more to sabotage their own results than all the bear markets and crashes in history.

Many economists have spent the last several decades telling us that humans are completely rational about their money 100 percent the time. That is crazy. For more than three hundred years, investors have had identifiable spells during which they were not fully—and sometimes not even remotely—rational.

Investment bubbles and crashes are the most obvious examples, but everyone can think of a time when he or she wasn't rational about money—just like some of those Iowans at the Younkers department store.

It's when our emotions are raw and close to the surface, even if we're not engaged in a world war, that behavioral quirks and idiosyncrasies are most likely to disrupt our allegedly rational financial plans. In *The Anxious Investor*, we'll discuss the dumb things investors do because of the behavioral biases we're all subject to. You'll learn why we're most likely to give in to these biases when feeling the stress of a bear market (a broadbased decline in stock prices of at least 20 percent). This means our biases do the most damage when things are already bad and we can least afford it. I'll examine these biases, putting them in the context of three stock market bubbles and crashes, so that you can understand how they might seem reasonable at the time. Then together, we'll study each bias without the context of history to fully understand them and learn how to avoid past investors' mistakes, because, unfortunately, none of the behavioral biases that humans display when investing—not a single one—generates better returns or minimizes risk.

This book is organized around those mistakes: fifteen of them, which the summary-oriented reader will also find in checklist form in the book's final section. But first, we're going to examine them by looking at the heat-of-the-moment experiences of investors during three especially destructive—and especially illuminating—episodes from financial history.

Chapter 1, "Fear," dissects the first financial bubble and resulting crash, and two of the most insidious behavioral biases.

The first is the disposition effect which is the tendency investors display when they sell their profitable investments and keep their unprofitable ones. Investors try to wrap this disposition effect in the flag of disciplined patience and lack of greed. All it does is hurt your investment returns. You'll also learn about loss aversion. Though it is logical to want to avoid losses, some investors take it too far and refuse to make advantageous speculations that have the odds on their side because the pain of losing is so much greater than the pleasure of profit. You'll also discover how gender impacts investing decisions and how the social aspect of investing, certainly today but also three hundred years ago, hinders success.

In the second chapter, "Irrationality," you'll learn by looking through the lens of the greatest stock price bubble of the last hundred years: the one in internet stocks that peaked in March 2000. It seemed the internet was going to change our lives, and it did. But some thought it would change theirs in a special way as whatever it was that made these companies and their fascinating founders so special rubbed off on them. It didn't work and we'll learn how fascination eventually gave way to disgust as prices collapsed. I'll show you how completely irrelevant numbers become mental anchors when we're trying to arrive at a reasonable estimation of a stock's value. We'll learn how the technology that was introduced during this decade made investing harder rather than easier, and how the flood of information brought some stocks to our attention just because they'd had an unusual move or traded an unusually high number of shares. Both might be newsworthy, but when investors consider only those investment ideas that are easy to recall, that are available to memory, then the resulting portfolio has the most newsworthy stocks rather than the best stocks.

Chapter 3, "Complexity," examines the Great Recession of 2008–09 which reminds us that it's impossible to see into the future even if it seems so obvious later. This hindsight bias, the belief that we saw it coming only because it is so vivid in retrospect, leaves investors overconfident that they'll see the next disaster before it unfolds. They can't. You'll also learn that although our world is becoming more complex, complexity for its own sake is merely confusing, leading many investors to look to others for a clue as to what to do. The resulting herding drives prices too high when times are good and too low when markets are under pressure. We'll learn about the related phenomenon of overreaction when investors are confronted by unexpected and dramatic events. We'll also learn that the attention we're able to pay to news and our finances is a scarce resource and that sometimes the well runs dry just when the ability to concentrate on our investments can generate the best outcomes.

Emotions cause humans to act strangely when money is concerned. When stress increases, as when the value of one's investments is being devastated by a stock market crash or a bear market, is when our disciplined efforts are most likely to give way to behavioral quirks we probably don't recognize in the moment. Our goal is to become a better investor by focusing on those times when it is difficult to be even a mediocre investor— when we're losing our heads during a bubble and during the nearly inevitable bear market that follows.

During times like this, our behavioral quirks are arrayed against us at the very moment we need to be at our best because that's when we can make a real, long-term difference. That's when better long-term returns—not good, perhaps, but better than our peers'—really matter. Understanding our behavioral foibles in these moments will help. It isn't that difficult to be a decent investor, the market will do much of the work for you. A single dollar invested in the Dow Jones Industrial Average (DJIA) on May 26, 1896, the day it was introduced, would have grown to $887.60 at the end of 2021. We can enjoy wonderful returns if we stay out of the way, even when the market seems to be at its worst.

These moments when the market is at its worst are inevitable. As of the beginning of 2022, the US stock market had experienced twelve bear markets since the end of World War II. Some were crushing—like the Great Recession that followed the collapse in our housing market in 2008 and saw the stock market decline by more than half. Some last for years, like the one that followed the bursting of the internet bubble in 2000. Fortunately, some have been shorter in duration and inflicted less pain on investors. No matter how devastating the results, we can safely say that bear markets are frequent; we experience one about every six years.

We've started to recognize the biases and marvel that we fall for them, but this is the first time they've been examined in the context of the worst sort of stock market. Up until now, they've been the subject of academic study in sterile classrooms without money and retirements at stake. We're going to look at them in their real settings: bear markets and crashes. Many books have been written about how to invest by examining the fundamentals of a company, or dissecting its balance sheet, or comparing its price-to-earnings (P/E) ratio with those of its competitors. Other books have been written about how to decipher the hidden meaning in a stock chart that has whimsical squiggles some call a "head and shoulders" or a "cup and saucer." But few have been written about why it is so difficult to execute our investment plan and so easy to get derailed just because the going gets tough. That's what we will examine. There are few places were these biases are laid bare like the old trading pits of Chicago's exchanges so in my decades as a trader on those floors I've witnessed, and personally experienced, every one of these biases. And in the coming pages, you'll get to benefit from that experience.

This analysis may be unpleasant at times because most readers will see themselves in the mistakes we discuss, but that is all the more reason to discuss them. Consider the money lost previously to be your tuition and the insight imparted by this book to be your diploma.

FEAR

He was an old man now. He had never been tall—he was so small and underweight at birth that he was not expected to live out the day—and at seventy-eight, he was stooped with age. His unusually small head did not add to his stature, but the silver-gray hair that fell to his shoulders concealed a formidable intellect.

His first name was almost certainly Isaac, although some say it may have been Lawrence, and a few say without much evidence that his last name was James. We know he lived in London in considerable prosperity, having accumulated a sizeable fortune for himself after turning from academia to finance twenty-five years before our story begins in 1720, a transition many have made since. In 1696 he had been named Warden of the Royal Mint, where one responsibility was investigating and prosecuting counterfeiters—at least two dozen were executed for the crime during his tenure. In 1699 he was promoted to Master of the Royal Mint and was paid £2,000 annually in salary and commission, equivalent to about $2 million today and about twenty times more than he had earned while teaching at university. He had no children—he never married—but maintained a comfortable household supervised by his half-niece.

After more than two decades as Master of the Mint, Isaac in 1720 had a net worth of about £30,000. Like many wealthy men his age, he invested conservatively. Most of his holdings were government bonds and shares of the few large, stable joint stock companies that were offered to the public. These included the Bank of England, which was founded as a private concern in 1694 to act as banker for the British government, and the South Sea Company.

Despite its fanciful name, the South Sea Company conducted a humdrum but immense and necessary business. In 1711, the British government had been groaning under approximately £10 million of debt (the precise amount was unknown) owed to creditors and contractors (the precise number was unknowable) who had supplied the British military during the War of Spanish Succession. The conflict had commenced when King Charles II of Spain died in 1700 without an heir. France and Great Britain maneuvered to fold Spain into their respective empires, battling for more than a decade at sites sprinkled across Western Europe. It was an enormously costly war.

The British government's financing of its various wars had always been haphazard because it lacked a unified budget and central treasury despite the scale of disbursements foreign war required. Each department would borrow and spend as it saw fit and the exigencies of a foreign war fought on multiple fronts which were separated by hundreds of miles, resulted in military quartermasters buying whatever materiel was needed to support the army in the field—on credit—at whatever prices were demanded and whenever it could be found. When the war limped to a close, four hundred thousand had been killed and Great Britain had spent £30 million, one-third of which was still owed to creditors a decade later.

The South Sea Company was formed as a private company in 1711 to help the government deal with the growing problem. The plan was for holders of government debt to swap their debt for shares in the company which would receive payment of interest from the government and pass it along to shareholders after keeping a small portion for itself. Each full share of stock would represent £100 in converted debt, and the shareholder would collect £6 in interest each year. Fractional shares were given to those who converted smaller amounts of debt. The share price would fluctuate around £100 as interest rates changed and as the £6 annual interest payment became relatively more or less valuable, but during the years immediately after conversion, the price of one South Sea share never strayed very far from £100.

The conversion of illiquid individual IOUs into readily tradeable shares was immensely attractive to investors despite the small percentage the company kept. The deal also promised to be a boon for the British government which would now deal with a single large creditor, the South Sea Company, rather than thousands of tiny ones. The government expected the arrangement would be so advantageous that it was anxious to get as many debt holders to go along as possible so it agreed to sweeten the deal; the company would be granted a monopoly on the potentially lucrative trade with South America—hence the name South Sea Company—and any profits from that trade would augment the interest payments made to shareholders.

Daniel Defoe, a well-known English journalist who published on a variety of topics including money and finance (despite having gone bankrupt in 1692 and spending at least two stints in debtors' prison), was typical of the many who were enthusiastic about the prospects for the company in light of the monopoly on trade with South America. In 1711 he wrote that the South Sea trade would "open such a Vein of Riches, will return such Wealth, as, in a few years, will make us more than sufficient Amends for the vast Expenses [*sic*]." Despite his previous financial misadventures, Defoe's hope, and the hope of all shareholders, was that eventually ships belonging to the company would deliver British manufactured goods to South American shores and return heaped with gold and silver from Bolivia, Mexico, and Peru, transforming the plodding business of collecting interest from the government and forwarding it to shareholders into a dynamic one focused on its monopoly on trade.

Unfortunately, the company's overseas trading was never very lucrative. The same treaty that ended the war also limited British trade with South America to a single shipload each year—and even then, the profit had to be shared with the new king of Spain. The only portion of trade with South America that the company could conduct without interference was the *asiento*, the right to import slaves from Africa. In addition to being grotesque, even that was never very profitable. Defoe would ultimately make out better in the South Sea. In 1719, he used the northeast coast of South America as a setting for his acclaimed novel *Robinson Crusoe*.

Its promise of great riches thwarted, the South Sea Company lumbered along, spending nearly a decade focused pleasantly on the business of collecting interest payments from the Crown and forwarding them to shareholders. It was profitable, if quiet, and since the British government had plenty of debt and little discipline in paying it back or avoiding the wars that spawned more of it, there was always additional raw material for the company to convert into shares.

More of that raw material was ripe for conversion in 1719. Even before the War of Spanish Succession, the Nine Years War with France, which had commenced in 1688, predictably drained the Exchequer and left it in debt. In 1694, Thomas Neale, the royal retainer responsible for organizing and supervising gambling in the court of King William III, hit on the idea of a "lottery loan" to cover the shortfall. Tickets cost £10 and winning numbers were drawn by chance. Every ticket holder got at least a £1 annuity for sixteen years and the luckier players would receive an additional annuity totaling between £10 and £1,000—an immense windfall in a time when a common laborer might earn £20 a year. That initial lottery raised £1 million through ticket sales, so Britain naturally did it again, and again. Between 1703 and 1715, another £10 million had been borrowed through lottery loans with similar terms.

Of course, Neale had not invented the lottery as a means of raising revenue. The Old Testament describes distributing land according to a random drawing and municipal governments in the coastal region of northwestern Europe, including modern-day Belgium, Luxembourg, and the Netherlands, had instituted lotteries to finance civic investment more than two centuries earlier. But Neale, who through his gambling post may have understood some of the general public's more degenerate impulses, would take it further than anyone had before.

It is likely easy to remember a moment when you were not completely rational about money. Nonetheless, the theoretical construct that economists latched onto in the 1950s, and which many still embrace stridently today, assumes that we remain rational. This concept conveniently does away with much of the computational messiness of economics, as qualitative issues such as idiosyncratic consumer preferences and John Maynard Keynes's "animal spirits" gave way to a purely quantitative, inhuman approach.

Prior to the 1950s, human emotion and frailty had been part of the canon of economics for hundreds of years. In the eighteenth century, Adam Smith, the Scottish economist sometimes called the father of modern economics, wrote not of capitalism but of "commercial society" which contained a healthy portion of human altruism. One hundred and sixty years later Keynes was the first to apply the old concept of animal spirits to economics. Acknowledging that financial speculation itself results in "instability," he went on to posit that there is also "instability due to the characteristic of human nature that a large proportion of our positive activities depend on spontaneous optimism rather than mathematical expectations, whether moral or hedonistic or economic. Most, probably, of our decisions to do something positive, the full consequences of which will be drawn out over many days to come, can only be taken as the result of animal spirits." Keynes defined animal spirits as "a spontaneous urge to action rather than inaction, and not as the outcome of a weighted average of quantitative benefits multiplied by quantitative probabilities."

Thomas Neale, the royal pit boss, understood this well. He created the lottery loan because it relied on sensation seeking, emotions, hope, and animal spirits—the urge to do something rather than nothing—to separate investors from their money.

When our minds are focused on some new, intense sensation, such as a bet or speculation that has the potential for profit, our brain releases a swirl of chemicals bringing about a blissful feeling. One of these chemicals is adrenaline which increases the heart rate which in turn increases the amount of oxygen reaching the brain. This enhances energy levels and mental focus. Another chemical released as a result of new sensations is dopamine, sometimes called the "feel-good" neurotransmitter, which contributes to a general feeling of happiness and pleasure. Others include the endorphins which ease physical pain and are responsible for the feeling of euphoria some feel after exercising.

We naturally want more of this feeling. Some of the activities that produce it, such as roller coasters, exotic travel, and horror movies, are harmless, while others, including illicit drug use, clearly are not harmless. Still others fall somewhere in between. These include drinking alcohol and trading on the stock market.

Economists have been confounded for decades by the volume of stock trading that takes place each day. In theory, the market reflects the equilibrium price for any stock at each moment in time. That equilibrium price should change, and trading should occur, only when something fundamental has changed for the company. This might be the announcement of an uptick in sales or the release of a new product—but those events are infrequent. Even if more frequent changes in interest rates drive some investors to change their opinions regarding the valuation of a stock, it should, in theory, experience trading activity maybe a couple dozen times a year. It would occur around quarterly earnings announcements, other corporate news, Federal Reserve meetings, and the release of macroeconomic data such as the unemployment rate. Instead, investors trade millions of times each day in volumes surpassing billions of shares. This trading cannot be explained by the economists who believe humans are purely rational. But it *is* logical if it is driven by "a spontaneous urge to action" or animal spirits.

One academic theory for this spontaneous urge is sensation seeking which is the tendency to pursue novel, intense, and varied feelings and experiences that are generally associated with real or imagined physical and financial risks. The quintessential examples beyond roller coasters, scary movies, and drugs are driving too fast and casino gambling. Given that the odds of winning are firmly in the casino's favor, the only logical rationale for gambling, euphemistically called "entertainment," is sensation seeking. We generally don't think of investing as a source of entertainment or thrills. But is it?

A study titled "Sensation-Seeking and Hedge Funds" examined the automobiles purchased by hedge fund managers and discovered many managers were sparked by sensation seeking when buying a car. According to the authors, hedge fund managers who owned high-performance sports cars took on more investment risk than their colleagues but did not generate commensurately higher returns. Even worse, funds managed by owners of high-performance sports cars were more likely to fail. These managers preferred unusual investment strategies such as investing in high-risk stocks that had a low probability of appreciation, appropriately called "lottery-like" stocks, and they traded more often. To be specific, hedge fund managers who drove sports cars took 11 percent more risk than hedge fund managers who drove minivans. These decisions make sense if you're looking for a thrill but not if you are striving for the best possible investment returns.

A study of driving patterns among individual investors in Finland from 1995 through 2002 demonstrated that those who incurred more speeding tickets were more likely to make stock trades. For each speeding ticket received by a subject of the study, the number of trades they executed increased by nearly 10 percent.

Maybe the best proof of the link between trading and sensation seeking comes from Asia. In January 2002, Taiwan introduced three new "Public Interest" lotteries with scratch-off cards, twice-weekly computerized games, and a bimonthly traditional lottery. They were seen as harmless fun in a country that loves gambling yet still outlaws casinos. Stock market trading in Taiwan declined by 25 percent when these lotteries were launched.

Trading stocks for entertainment naturally makes a game out of it. Investing shouldn't be an ordeal, but individual investors who do it for the thrill are likely to be less successful.

Sensation-seeking traders aren't crazy; they're just playing a different game than the deliberate, thoughtful investor who's trying to fund a child's education or their own retirement. Sensation-seeking traders are after the thrill, the shot of specific chemicals released by the brain, not the long-term accumulation of wealth.

Investors should ask themselves if they have a tendency to make a gamble of the market and trade for the sensation of it. If they do, they should remember this quote from Keynes: "The game of investing is intolerably boring and over-exacting to anyone who is entirely exempt from the gambling instinct; whilst he who has it must pay to this propensity the appropriate toll."

Thomas Neale's lottery loans were cloaked in the legitimacy of investing, but they raised so much money because of the titillation of the gamble. The thrill of a lottery loan, and hopes for one of the larger prizes, resulted in some individuals overextending themselves. But the lotteries at least paid high interest rates to ticket holders—compensation for the fact that the loans were paid out as an illiquid annuity rather than a lump sum.

With the thrill just a distant memory and the money spent by the government long ago, the lingering debt from Neale's lottery loans was another problem that could be rolled into the South Sea Company.

The 1719 conversion of lottery loans was even more successful than earlier efforts, including the original conversion of debt from the War of Spanish Succession. By converting the annuities into readily tradeable shares, the government was able to lower the interest rate it was obliged to pay. Meanwhile, debt holders received the flexibility of being able to sell their shares and cash out, rather than wait on the annuity payments.

These improvements did not go unnoticed. When stock traders were evicted from London's Royal Exchange for rowdiness, they started to gather at nearby public coffeehouses such as Jonathan's and Garraway's, both on Exchange Alley, a maze of walkways that opened across from the Exchange building and connected Cornhill Street, Lombard Street, and Birchin Lane. The three streets defined a lopsided triangle full of brokerages and banks that offered a ready clientele for the coffeehouse traders, adding a new social aspect to investing. One Londoner observed, "they that live in London, may, every noon and night on working days, go to Garraway's coffee house, and see what prices the actions bear of most companies trading in joynt-stocks." Investing, suddenly, was both salient and a social activity. Average investors (at least, those with the not-unreasonable sum of £10 and friends who frequented the coffeehouses), started hearing about the successful conversion of debt to equity in the South Sea Company and about the company's sparkling prospects.

Investors did not have to venture down to Exchange Alley and its coffeehouses to get the latest market news. They could instead turn to a new phenomenon: an independent press. By 1719, hundreds of newspapers and semi-regular pamphlets were fighting for readership, and those who did not subscribe could hear them read aloud in coffeehouses far from Exchange Alley. Several newspapers focused on financial news and published the latest prices each day with those for South Sea Company the most important.

The ability of investors to always know the value of their now-liquid shares was a new and profound contrast to the time when it had been impossible to know the exact value of their illiquid lottery loan annuities. Similarly, today it is easy to know the precise value of a stock portfolio—all an investor has to do is log into their brokerage account—while, in contrast, it is impossible to know the value of your home beyond some rough estimate. Precision in valuing one's holdings—and watching that value change from day to day—injected emotion and immediacy into investing in a manner that had never existed before. This precision also made individual investors overconfident regarding their understanding of the market, the profit they could expect, and their individual ability to realize it.

Prior to the creation of the South Sea Company and the ability of investors to convert their debt into shares, investors were never certain of the present value of their holdings but that was unimportant just as the current value of your home is relatively unimportant if you plan on living there another ten years. The illiquidity meant investors were essentially forced to hold their annuities and collect their annual payments. The South Sea Company resolved that uncertainty for the first time; not only was it possible to know what the shares were worth at any given moment, it was now possible to buy or sell at that price. This naturally made people wonder what shares might be worth next month or next year.

This uncertainty was both new in its specific form and ancient in general concept; today we would call it risk. The

English word comes from the Italian *rischio*, which has a generally negative connotation because it means hazard or danger, but it also refers to a venture that might generate a large reward. Risk itself was clearly not new, but the immediacy of this financial anxiety about current and future prices was absolutely novel for investors and it unleashed several of the subconscious biases and behaviors that often dominate the decision-making of investors under uncertainty.

The current price became an anchor when investors started to think about future prices regardless of the relationship to economic value. Investors started to give more weight to recent prices than longer term, base-rate prices when estimating future value. They started to look for, and find, patterns in prices even if they did not exist. Even the company's name, South Sea Company, generated emotions evocative of riches and romance.

For maybe the first time ever, financial engineering would lead the average investor to believe he had unlocked a valuable tool, but in doing so, it had opened a door into the turmoil and faults that make up the mind of the average investor.

The South Sea Company prior to 1720 was just the sort of stable investment a seventy-eight-year-old man like Isaac should own. It was boring but a good earner and it was easy to understand how money was made. Investors realized that the monopoly on trade with South America was not worth much—and the price of the shares reflected this reality—but there was a slight possibility that if events conspired and the relationship with Spain warmed, it might become very valuable. Events would indeed conspire in 1720 to make South Sea Company shares very valuable, though they had little to do with the South Sea or Spain.

Investors have wrestled with the idea of risk and how much they should assume even before Isaac heard about the South Sea Company. No one can determine the right amount of risk for you because everyone is different, and the general concept of taking less risk as your investment time frame gets shorter, while correct, is so vague as to offer little real help. One productive way to think about risk is to compare *tolerance*, which is the amount of risk an investor is willing to take, to *capacity*, or the amount of risk that investor is able to bear. They are very different concepts and we most often think about tolerance. The crux of tolerance is that this level is reached when we are most anxious, meaning when we're in the middle of a bear market or crash. Tolerance is most impacted not by how much the market is down but by how susceptible an investor is to the behavioral biases we'll discuss.

So when it comes time to define your risk tolerance, begin by going to the bias checklist at the back of this book and answer the questions posed there. Do you succumb to the biases? By how much? You'll begin to answer the question of how much risk you can tolerate by analyzing where you are in your investing life, but the next step should be an honest examination of how susceptible you are to these biases. If you are free from their influence then you're able to take more risk because you won't sabotage your own results just because the pressure of a bear market is weighing on you. If you are likely to fall prey to them, then you should assume less risk because it keeps you from getting into situations, such as facing a sizeable loss, when the biases can be particularly damaging to investment results.

One example is loss aversion; if you're able to keep from throwing in the towel and selling everything at the bottom then you've avoided loss aversion and had an appropriate portfolio for your risk tolerance. But if you're not able to discipline yourself and have the tendency to sell at the bottom, then you should modulate your risk so that capitulation doesn't become likely. The same is true for the disposition effect; if you tend to sell your winners just to have some good news when things are bad, then you should take less risk. We'll learn much more about both shortly.

Like many novel financial inventions, these conversions from illiquid debt to liquid stock had worked too well. In 1720, the British government took the conversion of public debt to private shares to its logical extreme. In January, the British Parliament began considering a vastly larger conversion. This one would total nearly £31 million—the majority of the remaining British government debt still outstanding—and this time Parliament would allow the company to sell extra shares for cash in addition to the shares that would be swapped for existing debt. The result would be to lower the interest rate paid to each share, but the company promised it would use the additional cash to boost earnings further. This would be good for the company but it was also necessary.

In 1720, the Bank of England was still a publicly owned joint-stock company. While it served as banker to the English government and to other banks, it was not yet the country's central bank and would remain outside government control until

1946. Having seen how lucrative the South Sea Company's previous conversions had been, the Bank of England decided to compete for this conversion mandate. Competition meant that the South Sea Company needed the cash from the sale of extra shares to pay the government £7.5 million for the franchise and to pay the bribes necessary to win the contract. Massive payoffs of both cash and stock were made to legions of government employees and members of Parliament, changing the complexion of the entire enterprise from staid to sordid and reckless.

While this latest debt conversion was being debated in Parliament, the company's directors and friends were talking up South Sea stock. They spread rumors that relations with Spain were improving and that the Spanish king, Philip V, wanted to exchange Spanish-owned ports on the west coast of South America for Gibraltar and for Port Mahon on the Mediterranean island of Minorca, both of which had been captured by the British during the War of Spanish Succession. Other rumors offered tantalizing but imprecise details of plans to eliminate restrictions on the number of trips British merchant ships could make to South America and abolish the taxes due to Spain. The rumors promised that soon "silver would become as common as iron."

South Sea stock stood at £126 when 1719 ended and Isaac had about 40 percent of his net worth invested in it. The company won the preliminary mandate for the £31 million conversion from Parliament in February 1720—thanks mostly to the extravagant bribes the company paid—and the stock closed that month at £179. The stock rose more in March to end the month at £220 as negotiations between the company and the government were being finalized. When Parliament voted on

April 7 to make the arrangement official, the stock closed at £320. It had more than doubled in just seventy-four trading days. Clearly, the valuation assigned to South Sea Company stock was no longer about the £6 per share annual dividend and was instead about the nebulous hopes for increased trade with South America.

As the latest conversion plan progressed through Parliament and as the stock price increased, the company was a frequent and bountiful topic for the army of pamphleteers at work in London. Pamphlets were a primary source of entertainment for the investor class in 1720, and, as with modern-day professional wrestling, much of the fun was the outrageous disagreements ginned up between rival authors. After all, the goal was to sell pamphlets, not to undertake meticulous analysis of any individual company. Unlike newspapers, which generally stuck to reporting prices, the pamphlets took sides with some touting the South Sea Company's prospects and trying to determine its value and some questioning how it could possibly be worth the astronomical sums being suggested given how vague the company was regarding its plans beyond the conversion of debt. When asked, the company refused to share even a rudimentary business plan.

Anyone trying to perform a rigorous quantitative analysis of the value of South Sea Company stock in 1720 was in uncharted territory. Not only was the company refusing to share its plans beyond debt conversion, there was no generally accepted framework for financial scrutiny. Various pamphleteers used a variety of valuation methods, which ranged from quackery to so astonishingly prescient that they closely resemble those used by today's most sophisticated investors. This fumbling about should be no surprise. Adam Smith would not be born for another three years and would not write *The Wealth of Nations*, the first cogent analysis of how a country's economy can grow and flourish, for another fifty-six. Even today, professionals routinely argue about the value of publicly traded corporations—and this is despite centuries of work refining quantitative tools and standardizing the data a publicly traded corporation has to release to shareholders. In 1720, the actual value of the South Sea Company was anybody's guess.

In this environment, the pamphlet with the most specific and detailed calculations became the most trusted. The *Flying Post* came out on April 9 and it mimicked one of the more sober broadsheet newspapers but it was published anonymously with the exception of an acknowledgment that it had been authored by a "friend" of the company. That friend was certainly a supporter and shareholder but was likely an employee, possibly even a board member. The treatise began with a review of the company's financial position as well as the public debt it intended to absorb and the interest payments it would receive and disburse. The tone of the review was suitably positive.

Then the writer took his reasoning a step further, asserting that since some were willing to pay £300, the shares were worth at least that much. In purposefully confusing price with value, he also engaged in some financial sleight of hand and argued that the shares were worth as much as £448 apiece. What his convoluted analysis failed to mention was that this was true only if you ignored the original shareholders and their claim to annual interest payments of £6 per share. In this way, the whole enterprise had become something like a modern-day Ponzi scheme. It worked only if you ignored everyone who came before.

This analysis relied on the fact that surplus cash would accrue to the company and remain in its account. It was a striking conclusion, and one that was heatedly discussed in the coffeehouses of Exchange Alley, where it was compared to the conclusions reached by competing pamphlets that tried to foment drama by offering their own valuation estimates. Isaac would have almost certainly heard the debate and read some of the rival pamphlets.

How much is a share of stock worth? That's really the question, isn't it? In 1720, everyone on Exchange Alley was trying to divine the future value of a share of South Sea Company stock. It was easy to know the price then, and it's even easier to find the price of a share of stock today, but it's never easy to know its long-term fundamental value.

Some say that the best measure is the sum of the future cash each share will throw off in the form of dividends and subsequent sale of the share. Cash received in the future would be discounted to reflect the time value of money ($100 in hand today is more valuable than $100 to be paid next year because, if nothing else, you could put today's $100 in the bank and earn interest on it), but since this is what the investor would receive for the investment they make today, it is a valid approach even if the precise timing of the payments is uncertain. If it's possible to know with precision the amounts and timing of the cash a company will return to shareholders, then this is a wonderful approach. It still leaves a few assumptions to be made. For example, what is the level of interest rates when that cash is paid out? Because $100 next year is worth less as interest rates increase and we could earn more money if we had the money in hand today. But it is difficult to know with any certitude the amount and timing of those future cash payments, including the eventual sale of the stock.

A common way to value a stock is to compare its price to the earnings it generates each year. This price-to-earnings ratio focuses instead on the profits the company generates for each share of stock outstanding rather than the payments it makes to shareholders. A higher price for each year's earnings suggests buyers expect earnings to grow, but sometimes the hopes for growth get ahead of the reality. There is no assurance that the company will continue to match its current earnings into the foreseeable future. Given how difficult it is to estimate profits beyond the next two or three years, it is folly to assume they won't decline sometime during the next twenty.

Likely the best way to value the South Sea Company was to simply treat the £6 annual payment as a perpetual annuity. If an investor was pleased with a 6 percent annual return, then each share was worth £100 to him. If he demanded a 10 percent annual return, then the value would be £60. Only if he was willing to accept an annual return of 2 percent forever did a price of £300 make sense. On April 14 the South Sea Company wanted to take advantage of the attention generated by the *Flying-Post* pamphlet while sharpening the social focus of the entire enterprise, so it tried a scheme so novel that it had been approved by Parliament only earlier that month: a subscription drive that allowed investors to pay for shares in installments. Previously, payment in full had been due when the shares were purchased. Now an investor could buy shares at £300—it is likely not a coincidence that the first hypothetical value mentioned in the *Flying-Post* pamphlet was exactly the price charged during this subscription—by making a £60 down payment and payments of £30 every other month until the shares were paid for. In all, £2 million in shares were offered and they sold out in less than an hour.

The share price jumped again, buoyed by this demand. A second subscription was offered and the share price continued to rally. Isaac decided to lighten up. He sold about thirty of his South Sea shares on April 19 and he would have realized somewhere between £300 and £320 per share, or a total of nearly £10,000.

At an April 21 meeting of South Sea investors, attendees heard vague presentations describing the company's plans. A strategy for growing the business would have been critical because its traditional practice of paying £6 annually per share could not justify the price it was commanding in the market.

We do not know what Isaac heard at the meeting on the twenty-first, but we know that the South Sea Company did not share a detailed business plan. We know this because it never had one. Two days later, Isaac decided to sell most, and maybe all, of his remaining shares, at nearly £350 each. He may have decided his shares were overpriced or he may have simply decided that this was enough for an elderly bachelor.

Isaac was demonstrating the disposition effect which is the tendency for investors to sell the winning stocks out of their portfolio and keep the disappointing or losing ones. The effect is a function of being human and our desire to experience the pleasure of realizing an investing gain while postponing the regret of realizing an investing loss. We are just not able to trick ourselves into achieving the maximum amount of happiness unless we sell. In one recent experiment, test subjects traded stocks while inside a functional magnetic resonance imaging (fMRI) scanner, which uses a strong magnetic field and radio waves to measure and map the brain's activity. When test subjects sold stock for a gain, they experienced a pleasurable spike in activity in the striatum, a clump of neurons at the base of our brain that is activated by rewards received in social settings. There was no pleasurable spike if the subject's stock went up in price but they chose not to sell. This helps explain why another study found that individual investors are 2.8 times more likely to sell a stock if its price has increased after purchase than they are to sell if its price has dropped. This happens despite every investor being told at some point to cut their losses and let their winners run.

In the other direction, the pain of regret from realizing a loss is greater even than the pleasure of realizing a profit. This asymmetry between pain and pleasure leads us to ignore the advice we're given and to instead let losers run while we cut short our profits. Although the disposition effect seems to be easy to recognize and correct, it is not unique to unsophisticated investors. Professional mutual fund managers fall prey to it as well, as evidenced by the tendency of a new manager who takes over an existing fund to sell losers at a faster rate than the manager who acquired them did. This is likely due to the fact that the new manager experiences no regret when selling her predecessor's losers.

Isaac and other investors who succumb to the disposition effect by selling winning stocks and holding losing ones are subconsciously assuming that investment returns will revert to the mean. That might seem to make sense after South Sea Company stock more than doubled from the end of 1719 to mid-April 1720, and investors might think they are being sober, disciplined, and are avoiding the harmful impact of greed. But even when stocks gain only a modest amount, investors tend to jettison winners more frequently than they cast off losers.

Another reason we can debunk the idea that investors are being their best selves when they're selling winners is because the tendency increases when prices are falling, as demonstrated in a 2021 study of nearly a hundred thousand German individual investors from 2001 to 2015. Researchers found that these investors were "25 percent more likely to realize gains in bust than in boom periods." If investors were just trying to avoid being greedy then we would expect the disposition effect to increase as prices rise. Instead, it increases as prices fall because investors who are watching the value of their portfolio dwindle are looking for a little good news and the only way to achieve that is to sell winners just when they become more important to the overall health of a portfolio.

There is also something beyond the pure brain chemistry of an isolated investor at work in the disposition effect. Social interaction, like the sort that was taking place in Exchange Alley coffeehouses, increases the effect. Today's users of social networks that focus on investing and trading exhibit individual disposition effects that are correlated to others in their network and the effect is greater than among investors who are not part of a similar social network. In some instances the effect is doubled among members of the network. Modern-day individual investors who live near one another also show correlated levels of the disposition effect.

Social interaction focused on investing and trading naturally increases the amount of trading participants engage in, but how does it increase the disposition effect? It is likely that the need to see ourselves as successful, and to enhance our reputation among others, encourages taking profits so we can brag to social media acquaintances and neighbors. This also discourages taking losses we might have to tell them about.

The disposition effect would be merely a charming eccentricity if it didn't have such a devastating impact on long-term investment results. One study of ten thousand brokerage accounts from 1987 through 1993 found that these investors were more likely to sell winners than losers and that the winners they sold outperformed the losers they kept over the following year by 3.4 percentage points. Another study of Japanese individual investors during that country's bull market from 1984 to 1989 was even starker; the stocks these investors sold outperformed the stocks they purchased by a total of 38.2 percentage points. The disposition effect costs investors money. And maybe even worse, the disposition effect tends to increase taxes that have to be paid. Capital gains taxes will be due on the gain from the winners sold, while tax loses, waiting to be harvested by selling losers, are squandered.

Traders who expect returns to revert to the mean are liable

to end up with a portfolio of loser stocks they hang on to and a few surviving winners they will sell too early. The disposition effect is easy to fall for, especially when we dress it up as a disciplined refusal to be greedy. But the effect is the manifestation of greed, the avaricious desire to fire the neurons in our brain that make us feel good—but only if we give in and sell our appreciated stock.

Why don't we learn? Learning in general is easiest when we're presented with many trials and immediate feedback. The quintessential example might be learning to ride a bike. We can get many attempts in an afternoon of practice and gravity offers immediate feedback. Many have offered the analogy that investing, when done correctly, is more like picking a spouse or choosing a career path than riding a bike; you don't get many trials and it may be decades before you have meaningful feedback. Plus, while we know how the stocks we still own have performed, we rarely seek out counterfactual feedback by tracking down the recent performance of stocks we have previously sold.

The best way to avoid the performance penalty inflicted by the disposition effect is to recognize that it's an emotional response, not a logical or financial one. Another way is to remember that successful investing is about what's going to happen in the future while the disposition effect is all about what has happened in the past. And as we'll learn, what happens in the stock market today has no impact on what it will do tomorrow.

By the first week of May 1720, Isaac had sold all his shares—they had been acquired over the course of several years at prices that were likely at or near £100. His total profits exceeded £20,000, roughly the equivalent of $20 million today.

He had sold his South Sea Company stock at a remarkable profit and invested the proceeds in government bonds, a wise choice for an old man. But South Sea stock continued to climb as the company introduced additional subscription schemes. At the end of May the price touched £400.

In early June, the company announced a third subscription which was scheduled for later that month. This one was the most outrageous; shares would cost £1,000 each, the down payment was just £100, and payments were spread over a five-year period.

During the second week of June, the share price jumped from £530 to £595 to £720 then £750. Isaac would have been aware of every uptick. Discussion of the South Sea Company was everywhere. One Dutchman, after returning home from London, reported: "The South Sea Company is continually a source of wonderment. The sole topic of conversation in England revolves around the shares of this company which have produced vast fortunes for many people in such a short space of time." The Irish satirist Jonathan Swift wrote, "I have enquired of some that have come from London, what is the religion there? They tell me it is South Sea stock. What is the policy of England? The answer is the same; what is the trade? South Sea still; and what is the business? Nothing but South Sea." Isaac would have heard all of it.

It should be no surprise that fraudsters saw an opportunity in the midst of this frenzy and the number of new enterprises soliciting investors exploded. These new companies were all dubious and most were likely fraudulent from their very inception, but they took advantage of the unthinking euphoria that had been sparked by the rally in South Sea shares. As a group, they were appropriately called "bubble companies" or simply "bubbles," and on May 7, 1720, before South Sea peaked, the *Weekly Packet*, a London newspaper, noted that "many of these projects are so ridiculous and chimerical that it is hard to tell which is most to be wondered at, the impudence of those that make the proposals, or the stupid folly of those that subscribe to [invest in] them."

Just five new companies were floated that January but twenty-three were launched in February and a stunning eighty-seven opened in June as the South Sea frenzy peaked. One of these new businesses promised investors it would make money by trading hair. Another wanted to extract silver from lead. One promised to profit from perpetual motion and was valued at £1 million. Yet another claimed it could cure venereal disease. James Puckle, a London inventor and lawyer, raised subscriptions to finance production of his Defense Gun, an early form of the machine gun. Its most unique feature? The weapon would fire round bullets at Christians and square ones, thought to be more deadly, at Muslim Turks.

The most daring of these entrepreneurs proposed the "carrying on an undertaking of great advantage, but nobody [is] to know what it is." In his 1841 book *Memoirs of Extraordinary Popular Delusions and the Madness of Crowds*, Scottish journalist Charles Mackay says this entrepreneur published his notice and the next day opened an office on Cornhill Road, hard abreast of the coffeehouses. He offered, by subscription, shares for £100 each and guaranteed a mind-boggling £100 annual dividend.

The down payment was a mere £2 with the balance due in one month. The founder sold subscriptions for a thousand shares and pocketed £2,000 in deposits during the five hours his office was open. He fled to Europe that evening and disappeared.

A total of 190 bubble companies were launched in 1720. Just four survived for more than a few weeks. It was a pattern that would be repeated with the dot-com boom in 1999—but we will come to that in the next chapter.

The problem for the South Sea promoters was that these bubble companies were drawing attention and investors away from the main game. If £2,000 was stolen and spirited away to Europe, that was money that could not be used to buy South Sea shares. Likewise, the £1 million that was chasing perpetual motion wouldn't be going into the South Sea Company's coffers. In early June, a bill to prohibit the formation of these bubble companies was introduced in Parliament and this "Bubble Act" passed almost immediately. Beginning on June 9, the formation of any new company required an act of Parliament, which the South Sea allies would never give, and existing companies were no longer allowed to operate outside their existing charters, something all the existing bubble companies did. The South Sea Company was once again the only game in town, and its shares would rally 50 percent during the next six days.

As Isaac watched this rally, the pressure to do something rather than nothing—Keynes's animal spirits—finally became too much. His better judgement gave way to emotion and he decided to buy his shares back as he focused on the recent action and extrapolated to even higher prices. Usually, the best thing an investor can do is nothing, yet Isaac could not simply stand by once emotion had taken over. A former cashier of the South Sea Company would later defend himself against charges of fraud by saying that many buyers of South Sea stock, and the stock of the bubble companies, bought shares even though "many of those very subscribers were far from believing those projects feasible; it was enough for their purpose that there would very soon be a premium on the receipts for these subscriptions when they generally got rid of them in the crowded [Exchange] Alley to others more credulous than themselves." This likely applied to Isaac as he watched prices advance and regretted having sold. Regret is an intensely powerful emotion, particularly so for investors.

Isaac may have believed South Sea shares were overvalued; after all, he had sold all he owned just two months before at much lower prices. Now he must have believed that prices would rise still further because he ignored the long-term historical returns for South Sea shares, which paid £6 a year in interest, as well as the annual yield of less than 0.8 percent in perpetuity if the shares were purchased for £770.

On June 14, Isaac sold the government bonds he had bought with the proceeds from selling his South Sea stock in April and May. Then he paid £26,000—most of his liquid wealth—to buy back in. South Sea stock cost £750 on June 15 and Isaac would have paid about £770 a share, double what he had received nine weeks before and 45 percent more than the price from the previous week.

This is how we know Isaac wasn't being admirably disciplined when he sold all his South Sea stock, that he wasn't a purely rational actor. If discipline and independent analysis had motivated his selling in May then he might have watched this frenzy with disbelief but would have been confident that the true value of the shares had not doubled in less than a month. He would have been confident that the market price and the long-term value had diverged, as they sometimes do. Instead, Isaac became a rank speculator rather than an investor, giving into his fear of missing out—or "FOMO," in the parlance of millions of traders who, three hundred years later, would embark on a similar journey with a handful of "meme stocks," such as GameStop and AMC.

Isaac initially felt he had done well. Shortly after he made his purchases, the company's books were closed and sales halted to allow it to reconcile accounts and pay the interest due to shareholders. When they resumed a week later, the pent-up demand and frenzy generated by the third subscription drove the price to £950. It seemed Isaac had made the right decision. He continued buying.

At this point, the total market capitalization of the South Sea Company—that is, the number of shares outstanding multiplied by the price of each share—was five times the total gross domestic product (GDP) of Great Britain. Today the total market capitalization of all US publicly traded companies combined, is less than two times our total GDP. Nobody buying South Sea shares could have thought he was getting a bargain. It would have been simply impossible to justify the current valuation. The only investment thesis that would have made any sense was to rely on the idea that a greater fool would come along tomorrow.

Isaac had become overconfident in his investing acumen and it would ultimately cost him dearly, just as overconfidence costs investors today. Overconfidence is sweeping in its scope. We tend to be overconfident regarding what we know, what we are capable of, how we analyze information, our ability to discern patterns in a sea of randomness, and what our future looks like. In short, we're overconfident when it comes to just about everything that makes us human, from the ordinary, to the profound, to things we have no control over.

In the realm of the ordinary, by definition only half of US drivers have above-average skill behind the wheel, but 80 percent of us think we are above-average drivers. Drivers are overconfident regarding their ability but much of what happens on the road is beyond our control. Despite this, even drivers who consider themselves ordinary believe they are less likely than most to be involved in an accident. These drivers are overconfident, but not regarding their ability. They are overconfident about the amount of sheer luck they will have on the road. Much of this self-deception regarding luck and the likelihood of being involved in an accident is a function of overestimating the degree to which we control our own fate. You may be the best driver in the world but that can't protect you from the bad luck of encountering a drunk driver (who probably believes that they possess above-average skill) who drifts across the centerline into oncoming traffic.

This illusion of control begins early—kindergartners exhibit it when playing games of chance—and while it tapers as we get older, it never disappears entirely so that most college undergraduates believe they are less likely than their roommates to develop cancer or suffer a heart attack before the age of fifty. This illusion also leads new parents to overestimate their likelihood of having gifted children and causes us to underestimate our chances of becoming victims of crime even though our ability to control these outcomes is limited by many factors including genetics and dumb luck.

This bias, believing we are more likely than most to experience positive outcomes and less likely to suffer negative ones, tends to be particularly high when (1) we have a strong desire for a particular outcome, (2) the probability of success is already high, and (3) we are convinced that we control the event, even if we do not. But likelihood of success is not required for the illusion of control to skew our assessment of the accuracy of our forecasts. This is evidenced by many people's belief that knowing the numbers drawn in previous lotteries increases their ability to pick next week's winning numbers or that they are more likely to win if they pick their own numbers rather than have them selected randomly. It's no coincidence that casinos post the winning numbers of recent spins of the roulette wheel, even though past results have zero predictive value. Casinos know that having that information makes players overconfident, leading to more and bigger bets. As weaknesses and psychological quirks are laid bare, dealing with money extends and magnifies our existential overconfidence.

Being overconfident when investing might be just another

quaint quirk—the sort of thing that endears us to our friends—if it didn't have a consistently pernicious impact on our investing results as it was about to do for Isaac.

Many people believe that becoming a successful investor is difficult—done correctly it doesn't have to be—but psychologists tell us that overconfidence is actually highest for complex tasks. That's the sort of counterintuitive finding that leads investors to let down their guard and allow their overconfidence to run unrestrained. This irony arises because those repetitive attempts—the essence of learning—means we also experience and remember the astonishingly full spectrum of ways in which things can go wrong.

Researchers tell us that there are two professional groups whose self-confidence is reasonably well calibrated to their actual abilities: meteorologists and horse racing handicappers. Both frequently confront problems that do not change much. Each trial generates objectively measurable outcomes and feedback is both rapid and specific. It will take just minutes for the handicapper to see if her horse wins while it may require just a few hours for the meteorologist to see if it does indeed rain. The absence of these conditions—experience, immediate feedback, and objectively measurable outcomes—breeds overconfidence. This describes investing: the best investors trade infrequently; feedback can require years; and even then, "success" is a subjective measure with dimensions related to broad market return, our investing goals, and the time until we need that money. Investing resists binary outcomes and that makes learning more difficult.

It is easy in an environment like this to fool ourselves into thinking we did better than we actually did. One way this happens is hindsight bias, or the tendency to believe that past events were more predictable than they actually were. As a result, we start to believe that future outcomes were obvious to us at the time, even if they were not.

On October 19, 1987, the Dow Jones Industrial Average plummeted 22.6 percent, the worst day the US stock market has ever endured. A few hours after the market closed, Yale University economist Robert Shiller, a future Nobel Prize winner in Economics, mailed a survey to 3,250 investors. The 991 responses he received showed that investors were convinced they had seen the crash coming. When asked how they knew, a number of them credited "gut instinct" but little of their objectively measurable trading confirmed that they had actually anticipated the collapse. The event was so striking, and the narrative leading up to it seemed so obvious *in retrospect*, that the respondent investors convinced themselves they had seen, or felt in their gut, the crash coming. Shiller's survey proved they were fooling themselves. The real danger of this hindsight bias is that it increased their overconfidence as investors because they had erroneously convinced themselves they could see into the future and would be able to sidestep the next crash or bear market.

Hindsight bias is another reason that complicated tasks generate overconfidence. For instance, when a marriage fails, it can seem so obvious in retrospect because it was often a single, albeit long process. Failure when learning to ride a bike happens in a smorgasbord of brief, discrete, unpredictable, and conflicting trials.

How else does overconfidence lead to poor investment returns? For one thing, it leads to investors holding riskier portfolios because they believe they are better able to interpret market action and thus they overestimate their savvy in bailing out before prices fall. In this way, they're similar to the investors in Shiller's 1987 survey who had allowed hindsight bias to fool them into thinking they could see into the future, even though they were not even able to accurately recall the very recent past.

Overconfidence fostered by the disposition effect and hindsight bias undermines investing returns. One of the most treacherous ways (and among the several Isaac was falling for) is overtrading. If you think a stock is worth $100 and it's trading at $50, you'll buy it; if you are overconfident in your abilities, you will be even more certain the stock is worth $100 and you may buy more of it. You have traded more and assumed more risk because of overconfidence.

What are the marks of an overconfident investor? The most obvious is gender. Psychologists have found that while both men and women exhibit overconfidence, men tend to be more overconfident than women and the difference is greater for tasks that are seen as masculine in nature. For many men, this includes investing. In an analysis of thirty-five thousand households with accounts at a large discount brokerage house from February 1991 through January 1997, men traded 45 percent more than women. This overtrading resulted in men's investing performance trailing that of women by nearly 1 percentage point (for example, 7 percent annual return versus 8 percent annual return).

If men are dumb, then single men are really dumb. A related study found that single men traded more than single women by

67 percent and subsequently had annual investment returns that were 3.5 percentage points lower than those of single women. The impact would translate to a difference of $187,990 after just twenty years for a $100,000 portfolio and average historical returns.

Being actively aware of the role of gender in the tendency toward overconfidence and overtrading is an important step toward investing success. How else might investors curb overconfidence? One way is to lose money. Investors who have generated substantial positive returns see their overconfidence increase as measured by the amount of relative risk they take, while those who have recently been losers tend to be relatively more risk averse. This is true even for those who didn't really make money but who rather tricked themselves into believing they had generated positive returns when all they really did was sell their winners and keep their losers in a cloud of disposition.

Another way in which overconfidence reduces investment returns is by skewing our understanding of risk. Overconfident investors will misjudge the likelihood of particular outcomes. They will believe that outcomes that are likely to occur, such as the stock market going up over time, are absolutely certain to occur and that outcomes which are unlikely to occur, such as a stock market crash, are impossible. (As we'll learn later, some investors who are not overconfident believe the opposite: that crashes are more likely than they actually are.) One study asked a group of test subjects a number of fill-in-the-blank questions on a variety of topics including history, music, geography, nature, and literature. After giving their responses, the participants were asked to estimate the probability that their answer was correct using a number from 0.00 (zero probability their answer was correct) to 1.00 (absolutely certain their answer was correct). When the estimate was 1.00, meaning the respondents were 100 percent certain they had the correct answer and there was absolutely no room for doubt, they were wrong 16.9 percent of the time. Now imagine feeling that degree of conviction about a stock trade. As the eighteenth-century French philosopher Voltaire wrote, "Uncertainty is an uncomfortable position. But certainty is an absurd one."

Isaac did not stop when he repurchased shares in the middle of June. On August 24, the South Sea Company launched its fourth and ultimately final subscription. Each share again cost £1,000 but investors had to put down £200 and fork over payments of £200 at six month intervals until the shares were fully paid. The shares now cost nearly ten times what they had cost the year before despite management offering no details about how it might transform the firm in order to merit that valuation beyond another enormous debt conversion. Nonetheless, Isaac subscribed for five shares totaling £5,000—the maximum available to any individual. He had likely now committed the vast majority, if not all, of his liquid capital.

Like most of the others, this offering was oversubscribed with investors demanding more shares than were available. Disappointed investors began complaining that the company's directors were favoring some well-connected buyers with allocations—the same allegation that would be made with lucrative IPO (initial public offering) shares 280 years later.

Isaac was now what would be considered by modern economists as a "noise trader." That is, his transactions were not the result of fundamental analysis of the company's prospects. They were instead driven by his confidence, or overconfidence, that stock prices would continue to climb based solely on extrapolating recent history into the future.

One critical aspect of these subscriptions is that they didn't just make it easier for investors to buy shares—they also dramatically increased the enthusiasm of pure speculators. Prior to the subscriptions, a speculator might buy shares thinking they would go up in value, but, like investors, he would have to pay in full. If prices went from £300 in April to £900 in July, then this speculator would have tripled his money. But if a speculator paid just £60 as the first installment of the first subscription in April and £30 as the second payment in June, then by the time the price reached £900 in July, his "receipt"—the contract showing how much he had paid and granting the option to continue paying and ultimately receive one full share—would be worth as much as £690 (the £900 value of one share less the £210 still due, although the buyer of the receipt was likely to demand a small discount). The speculator would have made not three times his investment but would have realized an approximately sevenfold profit. And if he paid installments in April and June, and then the share price fell, the speculator could simply refuse to make subsequent payments while, in a surprise move by the company, still getting a portion of the shares already paid for. This first subscription was not an agreement to buy the shares at £300 but rather it was an option. Since it was an option to buy the shares we would describe it as a call option. Call options like the ones offered by the South Sea Company generate enormous leverage, so they are popular with speculators.

At this point, Isaac was speculating; what he was doing certainly could not be called investing. Investing entails deploying money in the pursuit of gain despite risk because the investor knows the potential gain outweighs the risk given the time frame. Speculating, on the other hand, deploys money in the pursuit of risk in order to capture a short-term price change. The speculator is the gambler, the investor is the casino.

This was not the first time that the introduction of option contracts caused the price of a commodity to soar. The same thing had occurred in 1637 in Holland when the Dutch love of tulips and fascination with trading their bulbs generated new ways of speculating on their price. Dutch buyers of tulip bulbs had always agreed to buy them now and pay for them at some future point, but the agreement was an obligation. Beginning in November 1636, some traders began negotiating options: the right, rather than the obligation, to buy the bulbs in the future at an agreed-upon price. The potential buyer would commit just 3 percent of the purchase price but free himself from any additional risk. As a result, the speculative churn for bulbs exploded and prices rose twentyfold over the next three months. Modern-day options can be a wonderful tool for investors. But when they unleash the worst of our speculative impulses they foster bubbles and destroy wealth.

Each new subscription fed the social cyclone in Exchange Alley and drove prices higher. It is still common for even professional investors to be initially motivated to purchase a particular stock by some interpersonal communication with other investment professionals. In another survey, Professor Shiller found that "contagion of interest"—essentially, social interaction of the type that was going on in the Exchange Alley coffeehouses in 1720 and which would later take place in internet chat rooms and on social media—helps explain how institutional investors become aware of certain stocks with unusual price action. Shiller calls these stocks "boom" stocks. South Sea Company certainly would have qualified as a boom stock.

Isaac paid very close to the top as he continued his buying into July. Shares traded at £950 on the three days immediately after the company's books were reopened and sales resumed. This would be the high-water mark for the South Sea Company but Isaac kept buying, subscribing for the maximum number of shares allowed in the final subscription. In August the price sagged to £800.

As an investing proverb reminds us, "Nobody rings a bell at the top," so it is impossible to know the right moment to sell. In the same way, there is no way to know precisely why the South Sea bubble finally burst but, ironically, the Bubble Act, which outlawed competition from the bubble companies, is a primary suspect. The Act not only outlawed companies operating outside their charters but also granted the government the power to issue writs that forced businesses to show cause why they should not be disbanded. The potential for this drastic outcome terrified investors and they panicked, selling shares of the bubble companies for whatever was bid for them, no matter how low the price. Many investors were forced to sell even their South Sea shares in order to make good on their losses in the bubble companies.

People hate to lose money. We hate it so much that the very possibility of loss warps our thinking during bear markets such as the one that had just begun in South Sea Company shares. And the pain of losing money is more powerful than the joy of making it.

Paul Samuelson was the first American to receive the Nobel Prize in Economics and he helped change the discipline from the one Adam Smith and John Maynard Keynes had developed, which took into consideration human altruism, illogical failings, and animal spirits, to one that attempted to mimic the mathematical rigor of physics while ignoring the idea that economics is, at its heart, the study of how *humans* deal with money.

In about 1960 Samuelson was having lunch with some colleagues at the Massachusetts Institute of Technology (MIT), where he had become a full professor of economics at the age of thirty-two. Samuelson offered these economists an intriguing wager. Each of his fellow faculty members would flip a fair coin and call heads or tails. If the person called it correctly, Samuelson would pay him $200; if he was wrong, the person would pay Samuelson $100. This was no trivial amount as $100 then was equal to about $900 today. But the math was clearly on the side of his tablemates, and, besides, coughing up $100 would hardly have been catastrophic for an MIT professor. When Samuelson offered the bet to a professor he described as a "distinguished scholar," the man rebuffed him, explaining, "I won't bet because I would feel the hundred-dollar loss more than the two-hundred-dollar gain."

Samuelson, who advocated mathematical precision in economics, had demonstrated an illogical, emotional inefficiency;

humans are more averse to losing money than they are keen to make it. But Samuelson had also stumbled upon an interesting ratio between potential gain and potential loss. Subsequent research has shown that when people are offered a similar coin flip that would cost them $100 if they should lose, most will agree to play only if they are promised $200 to $250 if they should guess correctly. In other words, most people hate losing about twice as much as they enjoy winning, even when the stakes are relatively small.

This asymmetry, called loss aversion, makes some sense; each additional dollar has diminishing utility as we get more of them, and the less money we have, the more it hurts to lose each additional dollar. For example, a windfall of $1 million would be life changing for a family struggling with poverty (or to most families in America), but it would be relatively meaningless to a multibillionaire. This works differently in the other direction; the loss of each additional dollar hurts more than the one before it. Our hypothetical family, which now has $1 million, would feel the loss of $100,000. Losing another $100,000 would hurt even more and the pain would increase with each subsequent loss. Losing the tenth and last $100,000 would hurt most of all.

If you do not believe the utility of each dollar changes as your wealth increases, ask yourself which of these alternatives you would choose: a certain gift of $1 billion or the opportunity to flip a coin and win $4 billion if it comes up heads but nothing if it lands tails. Almost everyone would pick the first alternative even though its statistical value is just one-half that of the second. Why would most people make the "suboptimal" choice?

Because the utility of each subsequent $1 billion decreases significantly once you have the first $1 billion.

Loss aversion costs investors money. It may cause us to avoid reasonable speculations in which the odds are in our favor, like Samuelson's experiment, or profitable investments such as exposure to the stock market over a long time horizon. At some point, taking the certain rather than gamble for much larger sums, such as our $1 billion hypothetical example, does make economic sense, but the stock market never offers that sort of profile anyway. Instead, investing is a series of thousands of little decisions—many of which call for doing nothing—each of which has low stakes in isolation. It is when loss aversion, our tendency to be more sensitive to losses than to gains, is compounded that its impact becomes obvious even if we do not recognize it at the time.

Loss aversion leads investors to sell when the market dips because they have lost some money and the pain increases with each additional dollar lost. Making things worse, the many who suffer from the disposition effect sell the stocks which have performed best and remain above the level at which they were acquired instead of selling those that have performed badly and deserve to be liquidated. And then, rather than using the capital generated by selling to buy the bargains the market is offering, investors too often let the money sit in cash, idle, because the pain of losing more would outweigh the pleasure of a similar gain. This selling into dips and refusal to buy not only hurts long-term returns but it also sometimes creates a self-reinforcing feedback loop; the decline in prices generates fear among investors which makes them even more loss averse and more likely to sell, and less likely to buy, into the next leg of the dip, generating even more downward momentum. However, we have already seen that the stocks that are sold eventually do better than most. The legendary investor Peter Lynch sums it up nicely, "The real key to making money in stocks is not to get scared out of them."

Despite the thinking of economists who believe we remain completely rational, losses compromise the way we analyze markets and inhibit our ability to understand them. Our brains aren't very good at assessing loss in a nuanced way; we see the red figures and feel pain without differentiating enough between a modest loss and a potentially fatal one. It is only when a loss becomes unrecoverable, when it is nearly impossible to get back to even, that the investor's mind-set changes. In those situations, investors and gamblers change from loss aversion to risk seeking.

One example of this change in mind-set can be found among bettors at the racetrack. The racetrack is a wonderful laboratory for finance because all wagering is pari-mutuel—literally "among ourselves"—like in the stock market, rather than against the house at a casino. Plus, the stakes are manageable, emotions are loosed, and we get several trials each day. One consistent bias seen at the racetrack is the tendency for bettors to assign more value than deserved to longshots and less than deserved to favorites. After all, gambling is about sensation seeking and we get more sensation from a $2 bet to win on a fifty-to-one longshot than the same $2 bet to show on the even-money favorite. But that sensation comes at a cost. The average return for each dollar bet on a horse with odds of 100 to 1 or greater is 39 cents, while the average payoff on the favorite is 95 cents. Since the result is that too much is bet on the longshot relative to historical performance and odds, and too little is bet on the favorite, an economist would call this tendency a market "inefficiency." During the few afternoon hours spent at the track, one might expect the intensity of the effect to remain static but as the day continues and our bankroll shrinks—the victim of too many bets on too many longshots—this bias actually increases. It intensifies dramatically during the last two races of the day and is particularly prevalent during the final race, as losers try to get back to even by betting even more money on longshots, generally digging themselves deeper in the hole. Only when it seems that hope is lost do we fully let go of loss aversion, and then we do it in the dumbest manner possible.

South Sea prices continued to tumble in September 1720. On the eighth, it dropped below £700 for the first time since May and fell below £500 on the seventeenth, but loss aversion had not yet kicked in for Isaac. Instead, he remained overconfident that he was right and that South Sea stock would rebound—just as those test subjects were overconfident that they had answered correctly and there was not even one chance in a hundred they had gotten it wrong.

Isaac probably bought more in September although we cannot be certain beyond knowing that he was still optimistic about the company's prospects and that twice during September a trust which benefited the son of a friend, and for which Isaac served as one of four trustees, bought shares at approximately

£650 and then again at approximately £450. The closing price at the end of September was just £400. The share price had continued to tumble, partly because in the middle of the month, South Sea directors started betting against their own stock. By month's end, the company's bank had failed, crushed by loans it had made that were secured by South Sea stock. One writer attributed the undoing to the first leg down in July which brought a "prodigious number of sellers to the market; one man selling alarms another and makes him sell, and thus the stock has run down insensibly till all the people are put in a fright; and such has been the panic fear that it has brought great confusion along with it."

The extreme price action and precipitous drop had bankrupted nearly all the so-called South Sea men in Exchange Alley. A country gentleman who went to see the action wrote of one stockjobber (a stockbroker who also speculates for his own profit and loss) wringing his hands and wailing, "I am undone! I am undone!" Meanwhile, the five or six men around him where not offering consolation but were instead muttering, "So am I, so am I." In November, shares traded as low as £185, a decline of 80 percent from the peak in July after the company had reopened its books. The year had begun with South Sea Company stock at £128. It traded as high as £950 and the last two subscriptions sold shares at £1,000. The year ended with the shares at just £200. As for Isaac, he did not sell any of the shares he had reacquired.

Regret is stronger for decisions that result in action than for decisions that don't generate action, and our elderly investor was feeling regretful now. The danger for investors in the middle of a bear market is not that they'll lose money—that is inevitable at some point—but that the losses will be accompanied by regret which increases the intensity of the pain and makes it harder to act wisely. Just as we hate losing money more than we like making money, we hate regret more than we enjoy its opposite emotion, satisfaction. Even though it is easy to say that Samuelson's colleague should have taken his coin flip bet and felt no remorse if he lost—after all, the odds were on his side—the man was willing to refuse money, the $50 statistical advantage he was being offered, to avoid not just regret but also the knowledge that his having decided to accept Samuelson's wager had led to a loss.

Regret aversion theory predicts that investors will make decisions that reduce the likelihood of post-decision regret. This is distinct from avoiding losses; this is about avoiding regret. For example, parties to lawsuits will systematically choose to settle the suit not just because of risk, but because settling eliminates the possibility that they'll experience the psychic regret of an adverse verdict.

Why is regret so painful when it comes to investing? One reason is hindsight bias. What was uncertain at the time now seems obvious, so how could we have been so stupid as to not see it? The effort to avoid this feeling often leads investors to do nothing, even when there are logical steps to take, such as tax-loss harvesting, selling losers and putting the money into what is working (the opposite of the disposition effect), or putting free cash to work now that stocks are selling at a comparative discount. If you started with a reasonably constructed portfolio, then the right course may be to do nothing. Or it may be to own the experience and learn from it. The one thing *not* to do is to give into revulsion and shame; that can lead to selling at the bottom because of loss aversion or to status quo bias, which is the illogical tendency to prefer things stay as they are, even if making a change would prove beneficial. This feeling is common during a bear market and while we know now that it's not possible to time the market—to consistently buy the bottom of a move or sell the top of one—there are things that can be done to improve your investment performance. But this is also the time when investors are most overwhelmed and most vulnerable to the destructive behavioral biases that can torpedo their results.

The price of South Sea stock was disseminated to the public twice a day, at noon and at the end of the afternoon. The frequent updating of prices and the freedom to use that knowledge to sell or buy shares has a paradoxical result. Knowing that another price update is coming soon makes it easy to do nothing now. Rather than wrestling with the confusing roster of actions we might take now, we fool ourselves into believing we'll take action later. This is status quo bias. It has always existed because it's part of human nature to resist change even if it leads to a better outcome. Isaac was succumbing to it.

Status quo bias may be understandable but it's also expensive. For example, employees tend to stick with their existing employer-sponsored health plan even when cheaper and more comprehensive options become available. A little bit of time spent comparing their current choice to the newly available options would often be time for which they are well compensated. Yet few employees perform any analysis at all, let alone a rigorous one.

Status quo bias was also behind one of the biggest corporate blunders of the past fifty years. In April 1985, Coca-Cola announced that it would reformulate its iconic soft drink for the first time in ninety-nine years. Coke's CEO would say later that it was trying to "change the dynamics of sugar colas in the United States . . ." and was "taking intelligent risks." After all, Coke had been losing market share to the slightly sweeter Pepsi for fifteen years and the new, sweeter version of Coke, what the company came to call New Coke, was overwhelmingly preferred in blind taste tests of nearly two hundred thousand consumers. Coca-Cola believed it was giving the public what they wanted. But consumers howled, including some of those who actually preferred the reformulated version. The company became a laughingstock and the subject of general derision. One customer considered the decision so stupid he wrote a letter to the chief executive officer and addressed it "Chief Dodo, the Coca-Cola Company." By then, the decision was so infamous, even inside the company, that the mail room delivered the letter to the CEO's office.

Coca-Cola had a need to address; it was losing market share and had a "new" product that many of its customers preferred. So where did the company go wrong? By ignoring the power of status quo bias. Consumers wanted "Old Coke"—what came to be known as Coca-Cola Classic—because they disliked change even more than they liked a tastier cola. When it comes to investing, humans sometimes have an irrational preference for their current portfolio even if changes or alternatives would leave them with more money come retirement.

Isaac's finances would have been fine had he simply held the shares he owned at the start of the year; in fact, he would have enjoyed a nice gain of more than 50 percent. But as March 1721 approached, he was now facing a wrenching decision. The second payment of £1,000 for his subscription of five shares would come due on March 25. He could simply refuse to make the payment; his rights would lapse, and he would not receive any shares. (A subscriber had to make the second scheduled payment in order to get the portion of shares he had paid for; if he made only one payment, he lost the initial deposit.) He could pay and hope the shares rebounded but he would be paying five times what the shares now brought on the open market. Or he could sell his receipt to someone else at a discount and recoup at least a portion of his investment. This last option is what he did sometime between the beginning of March and the end of August 1721. We do not know what kind of discount was demanded by the buyer but it would have been sickening for Isaac. We know that he executed no other transactions in 1721 or the first half of 1722—he had no other winners to sell as part of the disposition effect, which he had already fallen for, and he would have hated to realize a loss, so he did not want to sell his South Sea shares. Sometime in mid-1722, Isaac finally began diversifying out of South Sea shares and into shares of the Bank of England when it offered its own subscription scheme. Those shares were fully paid up in January 1724.

Isaac's losses during the entire episode amounted to approximately £20,000, well more than half of the net worth he'd started the year 1720 with. His disgust was evident when a friend later asked him to invest in a company he was starting.

South Sea Company Share Price, August 1719 – December 1720

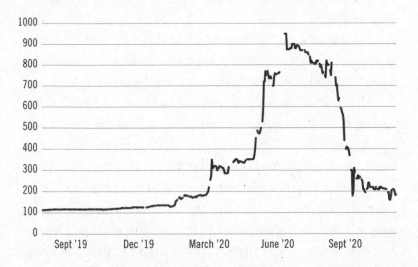

Isaac declined, writing, "I lost very much by the South Sea company which makes my pockets empty, and my mind averse from dealing in these matters." It is rumored that he told others he lost so much money he could not bear to hear the words "South Sea." And he had done it to himself, by giving way to the temptations that all investors feel, especially when a bubble is inflating and then coming undone.

It is common to search for scapegoats and there are almost always bad actors in these episodes. In December 1720, the directors of the South Sea Company were forced to provide a complete account of their "proceedings," and employees and leadership were prohibited from leaving the country for the next year as the investigation progressed. Their assets were attached so they could not be spirited away but a Mr. Knight, the company treasurer, disguised himself and fled for France with many of the company's documents. This was seen as evidence of guilt and King George I—who had been encouraged by insiders to sell his own South Sea shares near the top but refused—closed the ports that evening to prevent additional escapes by those responsible. But the investors carry blame as well.

Moods and emotions are enormously powerful because investing is a human endeavor despite what Paul Samuelson and his ilk would have us believe. There is a reason that the stocks listed on the New York Stock Exchange do better when the weather in New York is sunny than when it is cloudy. Or why stock markets in other countries do better on the days immediately following a big win for the national soccer team. Or why people buy more lottery tickets in Ohio in the days following a win by the Ohio State University football team. It is not because the Almighty is a fan of the Buckeyes.

Isaac was not the only one to get caught up in the South Sea bubble and, given some of his eccentricities, we shouldn't be surprised he got carried away in his effort to make even more money. By 1720, he had already spent long periods of his adult life in the study of alchemy, the search for the chemical process that would turn base metals such as lead into gold. When he was an academic, his classes were so poorly attended that sometimes no students showed up at all, yet he delivered his lecture as if the classroom were full. During a one-year term in Parliament beginning in 1689, he uttered only one sentence for the official record when he asked an usher to close an open window.

Despite this, Isaac's adventures with the South Sea Company should dispel the concept that investing is all about intellect. Although he was the only son of an illiterate farmer who died three months before he was born, Isaac would be entombed in Westminster Abbey, have his epitaph written by the famous English poet Alexander Pope, and be eulogized two hundred years later by Albert Einstein. Indeed, Isaac was likely the most intelligent person alive in 1720—and possibly the most intelligent human who ever lived. Because while some say his first name was really Lawrence and some say, without much evidence, that his last name was James, he was generally known then and now as Sir Isaac Newton. He invented calculus and devised the formula for universal gravitation. He discovered that light is actually made up of a wide range of wavelengths, with each one representing a constituent color of light. His book, *Principia*, described the foundation for classical mechanics including his three laws of motion. But when asked about his experience in the South Sea bubble, the renowned physicist and mathematician would say, "I can calculate the motions of the heavenly bodies, but not the madness of the people."

It might have been more appropriate for Sir Isaac to say the "madness of myself" because while he was swept along with the herd, he could have known better and he could have avoided the disposition effect. As we continue, we'll examine additional behavioral biases in the context of other bubbles and crashes. They will include investors becoming enthralled by transformative businesses the way some were swept up by the promise of the South Sea Company, certain it was going to change the old world by importing the riches of the new one.

Other investors bought South Sea shares because the company was the first to come to mind when thinking about investment alternatives. One observer said it was the only topic of conversation in London, and Jonathan Swift said it had become a religion for many. In the next chapter, we will see how some companies dominated the discussion in both broad society and among investors.

Many investors in 1720 became emotional about the prospects for the South Sea Company. Next we'll see how that happened again centuries later. And just as Isaac Newton felt revulsion whenever anyone mentioned the South Sea Company, we'll see how later investors feel the same emotions when their investments in transformative businesses fail.

It was Friedrich Schiller, the German poet and philosopher, who first said, "Anyone taken as an individual is tolerably sensible and reasonable; as a member of a crowd, he at once becomes a blockhead." In the next chapter, we'll see other examples of how this is so, while also describing ways to avoid becoming an unthinking member of the herd.

CHAPTER 2

IRRATIONALITY

NEI Webworld had nothing to do with the internet. As the internet bubble was nearing its peak in November 1999, Webworld didn't even have the dial-up internet connection available to everyone thanks to the ubiquitous discs that arrived unsolicited in the mail. It was instead a commercial printing firm that took its name from an eighty-year-old offset printing process that feeds a continuous roll of paper, or web, through the press machinery. In 1999, at the height of the internet bubble, NEI was the type of old economy company that seemed about to be put out of business by the Worldwide Web that Webworld had nothing to do with. But Webworld was already broke, having filed a voluntary petition for bankruptcy and liquidation on December 7, 1998.

Webworld stock still traded despite the company's bankruptcy, but just barely. It was listed and traded on the over-the-counter bulletin board (OTCBB), a netherworld for penny stocks and other shares of dubious quality that could not qualify for listing on, or had been kicked off of, a legitimate

exchange. In November 1999, six months after ceasing operations and liquidating all its assets, the desiccated corporate
husk of Webworld was trading for less than 20 cents a share.
Once the bankruptcy judge issued a ruling, the company would
be officially dissolved and its stock would cease to exist. Given
that, it was a mystery why anyone would pay anything at all
for shares of NEI Webworld but the over-the-counter bulletin
board was filled with companies even worse off. Much of the
attraction for these stocks was the sensation seeking that Isaac
Newton and other investors experienced in 1720. The stock of
Webworld might begin the day at 5 cents a share and triple by
the afternoon. It would eventually fall back when anyone tried
to sell shares; after all, the company was bankrupt and had no
operations. But speculators were enjoying the ride.

It was not just bulletin boards stocks that were rallying as
Webworld worked its way through bankruptcy court that fall;
legitimate ones were following a similar trajectory. The tele-
com company Qualcomm would see its stock price rise by 63
percent in November 1999 alone on its way to a 2,610 percent
gain for the year (the stock rose from $3.25 to $88.06). The
Nasdaq Composite Index is a measure of the prices of all the
stocks listed on the Nasdaq stock exchange and in 1999 it was
focused on technology and internet stocks. It gained 86 percent that year. American Online (AOL), the company mailing
all those computer discs to get you to sign up for their internet
service, would gain 94 percent.

Anything having to do with the internet and World Wide
Web seemed like a good bet in this environment. So too did
stocks that had nothing to do with the internet but appeared

that they might. That described NEI Webworld. In November 1999, two twenty-three-year-old friends, Hootan Melamed, a pharmacy student, and Arash Aziz-Golshani, who worked in the family business selling leather coats, started accumulating shares of Webworld. They would purchase a total of 130,000— nearly every share outstanding—at prices between 5 cents and 17 cents. Then they went to work.

Operating out of the UCLA biomedical lab in order to cover their tracks, they used fifty different aliases to post messages in five hundred internet chat rooms aimed at investors, while being careful to make their activity resemble legitimate conversations between knowledgeable and sophisticated market participants. They spun a tale of how another company, LGC Wireless, was going to acquire Webworld. In a stock market where it seemed everything that had to do with the internet was soaring, who was to doubt that something called Webworld would soar as well? After all, a similarly named company, Webvan, had gone public earlier that month and gained 66 percent on its first day in a story that was both outlandish and typical for the time. Webvan's business was nearly as much a part of the old economy as Webworld's had been. It planned to provide online grocery shopping and delivery, and while the online ordering portion of the business model was novel, grocery delivery was nothing new; kindly neighborhood grocers had been hiring local teenagers to do it for decades.

Webvan projected it would initially operate in just ten American cities but even with those modest plans, the company had almost no active operations when it went public. It would generate just $400,000 in total revenue during the final three months of 1999—about what a single average-size supermarket would gross every two weeks—while piling up losses exceeding $50 million. Yet on the day of its initial public offering, when a few lucky individuals were able to buy shares at just $15, it opened for everyone else at $26, then rallied to $34—it seemed every internet stock traded dramatically higher on the morning of its IPO—before closing at $24.88 a share, giving Webvan a valuation of $7.9 billion. If Webvan merited this sort of valuation, then why not Webworld?

In one of their chatroom messages, Hootan and Arash urged investors to buy Webworld because, "People who know of the deal are buying in, given the large volume in the last few days." What they did not say was that their own buying was responsible for the surge in volume, but thanks to their clandestine work a buzz was building among readers who were logged on. On Monday, November 15, those readers became buyers. Webworld shares had closed the previous Friday at 13 cents but opened for trading on the bulletin board at $8. Hootan and Arash started selling. Fifteen minutes later, shares were trading at $15.31. The two were still selling and that killed the rally just as selling in the past has killed other rallies. A half hour later Webworld was back at 25 cents a shares. Hootan and Arash had made a profit of $364,000.

The crime was not particularly sophisticated so it didn't take long for regulators to unravel who had originally purchased the shares, who had posted the fake rumors, who had sold the shares, and who had made the money—or the fact that they were the same two people. Just thirty days later, on December 15, the United States government indicted Hootan and Arash on three counts of securities and wire fraud.

Irrationality

In the supreme example of just how screwed up the stock market had become at the end of 1999, word of the charges sent the price of Webworld shares soaring again, even though press reports described it, accurately, as a "bankrupt Dallas-based printing services company." Webworld had opened for trading at just below 19 cents a share on the day the indictments were announced. After the announcement, it traded as high as $2.38 and closed at 31 cents, a gain of 67 percent—almost identical to the gain for Webvan on the day of its IPO. How could this be?

Webworld had a name that seemed vaguely related to the internet and had come to the attention of investors if only because it was the vehicle for securities fraud perpetrated by a couple of twenty-three-year-olds. One buyer who paid just over $2 a share that day said later, "Every other second, the thing was going up, up, up. . . . I thought, *I'll jump in and out*." He never did "jump out" and still owned his shares when the market closed that day.

The internet boom introduced investors to an astonishing array of new products that seemed miraculous and that actually changed lives. Just try to imagine what life would be like without the internet browser or email. We'll see how some investors internalized their relationship with the fantastic new products being introduced and the fascinating entrepreneurs who were introducing them.

The internet, and the tools to connect to it and use it, were initially free. In the late 1990s it was still largely free and there remained a deeply-held bias among the cognoscente against commercializing it. Entrepreneurs who considered that outlook to be outdated and silly, and who were trying to make money on the internet, like those who had started Webvan and taken it public, still had not figured out how to do so in November 1999.

The internet was developed in the 1970s by the US Department of Defense to not just embrace anarchy but harness it. Amazingly for something created by the Department of Defense, there was no central authority. Theoretically, anyone could connect to the internet—although it was originally intended as a way for academic researchers to access the few and far-off supercomputers, and to share research. What made the internet work then, and what continues to make it so versatile now, is not a rigid architecture but a technical protocol that allows any two computers to communicate without the sort of fixed circuit that a telephone requires. The internet instead sends "packets" of data that are forwarded to the recipient's address by whatever node an individual packet happens to pass through. This lack of central control means the packets will reach their destination even if a portion of the network fails. It was this capability that intrigued the Department of Defense.

The idea of using the internet for commerce would not have occurred to anyone when it first went live. It was an academic tool, and though the concepts that made it work were elegant, the entire process was fabulously complex. Using the internet to access a supercomputer or share data required intimate knowledge of the computer languages and programming syntax that made their masters modern-day Egyptian scribes.

The original version of the internet was like a magical hallway that opened onto different rooms. Some housed supercomputers while others stored mountains of data that researchers would stitch together in their chase to answer the fundamental questions about our universe. But by 1989, the growth of different computing platforms, operating systems, and applications meant many of those doors were locked to a researcher who didn't have a particular key in the form of the corresponding computer language or platform.

Tim Berners-Lee was a physicist working at the European Organization for Nuclear Research (CERN) in Switzerland. CERN, with its particle accelerators, massive computers, and legions of scientists was the sort of facility the original internet was meant for. But Berners-Lee realized the initial promise of the internet had been overwhelmed by the explosion in proprietary technology. In 1989, he suggested to his boss that CERN develop a network which would manage all these resources and allow users to access them via a common hypertext computer language, essentially a skeleton key. According to Berners-Lee, his proposed network, originally called the Mesh, would make every information system that was connected to it look like "part of some imaginary information system which everyone can read." The Mesh eventually became the World Wide Web.

Still, the Mesh remained a tool for CERN's scientists and no one thought of using the Web for commerce. The people who were logged on were trying to figure out what had happened in the moments after the Big Bang, not how to make a billion dollars. To foster that search for answers and hasten adoption of the Web, CERN decided in April 1993 to put the World Wide Web into the public domain, making it free, to everyone, for anything, forever. This egalitarian spirit was laudable. It would also handicap everyone who came in the next few years and wanted to use the Web to make money.

The Web was now free, and it was easier to use than the original internet, but it was not yet *easy* to use. Berners-Lee's hypertext was daunting even if it was the only language anyone had to master. It worked more like a typewriter than a real computer because it displayed a single line of text at a time, and even then, it worked only on NeXT brand workstations built by the company Steve Jobs had founded after he got fired from Apple.

CERN was not the only place made for the internet and Tim Berners-Lee was not the only one who realized the internet was a failed promise. Marc Andreessen was a computer science major at the University of Illinois who worked part-time at the university's National Center for Supercomputing Applications. Andreessen realized the Web was an improvement for researchers but there were still barriers for those who wanted to focus on science, not on learning the hypertext language the Web required. So, he set out to build a program that would bring the point-and-click functionality that Apple and Microsoft had been using for years to the interface between a user and the Web.

Andreessen's Mosaic Web browser was released early on the morning of Saturday, January 23, 1993, and it was a point-and-click revelation. Web users no longer faced a green phosphor screen with a blinking cursor or needed to execute a dozen precise keystrokes merely to open a program. A *New York Times* headline about Mosaic grabbed readers' attention, "Enormous Stores of Data Are Just a Click Away." It called the browser "an applications program so different and so obviously useful that it can create a new industry from scratch." Mosaic be downloaded several hundred thousand times by the end of the year, and it opened the internet to so many all at once that internet traffic overwhelmed network capacity. And, consistent with the researchers' ethos, it was free.

Even after Andreessen graduated, moved to Silicon Valley, and went to work for legendary entrepreneur Jim Clark building a new Web browser at what would become Netscape Communications, he was determined that Web browsers—and, really, everything about the Web—remain free to users. This novel concept was unique to the internet; other software wasn't free, and nobody expected it to be. When Andreessen and his team of programmers completed their new Netscape browser, one colleague suggested charging $99 for it. The number of downloads of Mosaic had proved there was a market for a browser and Netscape's version, fittingly named Navigator, was vastly superior to Mosaic. Given the power to open the Web and the glowing review of Mosaic in the *Times*, $99 would have made Netscape's browser a bargain.

The company was certainly no charity. Clark, having fronted all the initial capital, which amounted to several million dollars and a significant portion of his net worth, needed Netscape to be profitable. But when he asked himself how Netscape, or any company, might make money on the internet if everything were free, he would later write, "I didn't have a specific answer to that yet, but I figured that with the Web- and Mosaic-enabled internet already growing exponentially, you couldn't help but make money. It was just the law of large numbers at work—even a small amount of money per user would yield a big business."

In a press release issued on October 3, 1994, Netscape announced that it was "offering its newly introduced Netscape network navigator free to users via the internet" and quoted Andreessen: "Making Netscape freely available to internet users is Netscape Communications' way of contributing to the explosive growth of innovative information applications on global networks." It certainly did that, but Navigator wasn't generating even the pittance per user that Clark believed would make them all rich.

Netscape Navigator could take casual users anywhere they wanted on the Web for free. But where to go? Many of the people using the new Netscape Navigator were going to Yahoo.

Yahoo started as a simple online list of websites that two Stanford University electrical engineering PhD graduates found useful. Jerry Yang and David Filo started the list in February 1994 when they were supposed to be working on their dissertations, but by autumn, it was getting a million hits a day and had nearly a hundred thousand unique visitors—a measure of both the growing popularity of the Web and its dearth of content. The two soon shortened the initial name of their list, *Jerry and David's Guide to the World Wide Web*, to Yahoo.

Yahoo was a logical starting point by the time Navigator was released. The internet portal offered news, finance, sports, and an early, crude, search engine. Yahoo kept visitors from wandering off to other sites by becoming "sticky" through the addition of email, games, weather, and maps.

The internet bubble really got going in 1995 as entrepreneurs tallied the number of Americans on the internet thanks to AOL and Netscape and realized those twenty-five million people constituted a huge market. Some of the new rooms that opened off the hallway that was the Web started trying to sell stuff. Amazon.com opened for business in July as an online bookstore. eBay opened just after Labor Day as a hobby project called AuctionWeb on the personal website of Pierre Omidyar, a former programmer at Apple Computer. Omidyar's goal was to build a site that would "bring together buyers and sellers in an honest and open marketplace." In sympathy with the Web's original spirit, eBay was initially free to users. Omidyar eventually began asking sellers to mail him a check as a commission to offset his expenses but the whole thing operated on the honor system. When enough checks arrived that he had to hire someone to handle the mail, he turned his hobby into a full-time job.

Despite the fact that Netscape wasn't selling anything or generating any profit, its shareholders were making money. The company went public in August 1995 at $28 a share, closing on that first day of trading at $58.25. By year's end, it was trading at $139 a share.

John D. Rockefeller, the founder of Standard Oil Company, was once the most hated man in America. By setting out not merely to beat competitors in the oil and kerosene market, but to crush them by relentlessly lowering prices below their cost of production, he threatened to humiliate and ruin them if they didn't sell out to him on terms he dictated. Rockefeller ended up controlling the market that made it possible to strike a match rather than curse the darkness. In doing so, he became the richest man in America and by many measures the richest self-made man of all time.

Internet entrepreneurs of the 1990s could have been just as hated. They were taking the internet, which had been initially funded by taxpayers, and were trying to make a buck off it. The magnates who ran most of the software and hardware platforms had created proprietary ecosystems that didn't work with other platforms and once a user committed to either Microsoft Windows or Apple, those businesses often charged accordingly. Taking a page from Rockefeller, some chose not to charge at all—not out of allegiance to the Web's egalitarian beginnings but to build market share and crush their competition. The Web was still seen as more novel than necessary, so the implications of these sharp-elbowed tactics were lost on casual users who were enthralled rather than enraged.

Some who had not logged on yet were cowed by the technical complexity they assumed was lurking, so they derided the whole thing but, surprisingly, spared the programmers who made it work. Those programmers were the pasty-faced kids who had been ridiculed in high school, and it would have been easy for that scorn to evolve into something more caustic as envy over their riches intruded. Yet, as average Americans became aware of the internet and started to explore it, they weren't cursing the magnates and most managed to get past any intimidation of the complexity. They were instead enchanted by where it took them and by the people who made it possible. The first time most Americans saw a photo of Marc Andreessen was when he appeared on the cover of *Time* magazine on

February 19, 1996, dressed simply in a casual black shirt and jeans—and barefoot—while posed on a gilt throne. The cover described him as an "instantaire," in reference to the money he'd made from Netscape's IPO. The hated Rockefeller never appeared in public unless he was wearing a jacket and tie and nobody outside his household could have imagined seeing him in the sort of every-man clothes, let alone barefoot, the fascinating if not yet beloved Andreessen was wearing on the cover of a national magazine.

As more internet-based businesses were created, founders became celebrities in a way that was previously rare for entrepreneurs and almost impossible for CEOs who were mere managers of existing businesses. Apple cofounders Steve Jobs and Steve Wozniak were household names by 1995, as was Bill Gates. Jobs first appeared on the cover of *Time* in 1982, when he was twenty-six years old, then again in 1997 and 1999; Gates first appeared in April 1984 and appeared about once a year from June 1995 through 2000. One 1995 cover boldly anointed him "Master of the Universe" and said he had "Conquered the world's computers," just as most Americans were discovering the internet. Steve Case, AOL's CEO and chairman, appeared on the covers of *Time* and *Newsweek*. Jeff Bezos, founder of Amazon, was *Time*'s Person of the Year in 1999. Other readers fell for the adorable story of how Jerry Yang and David Filo had founded the most famous website of all, Yahoo, while conveniently forgetting they were PhD students in the most prestigious computer science program in the world.

Two other Stanford graduate students, Larry Page and Sergey Brin, became well known for wondrously advancing the efficacy of internet search when they launched Google in September 1998. People used the platforms Andreessen, Jobs, and Gates had created to access Bezos's Amazon, Brin and Page's Google, and Filo and Yang's Yahoo, and investors also bought the stock of the companies those entrepreneurs had founded. This affinity for founders, companies, and platforms would end up becoming dangerous for investors as they formed emotional attachments and embraced the feeling that some of what made these founders and their companies special could rub off on them.

This new version of celebrity was fueled in part by the stock market. The Nasdaq Composite nearly tripled from the end of 1994 to the end of 1998 and gained at least 20 percent each year during that stretch. Microsoft gained 808 percent during that period. Yahoo gained 5,368 percent from its IPO price to the closing price at the end of 1998, and AOL, the company making it possible for 60 percent of all Americans who were online, gained 8,764 percent after accounting for five stock splits during the period, including two in 1998 alone. The founders of these companies were now both rich and famous.

As we learned from the story of Sir Isaac Newton and the South Sea Company, even the most analytical humans are not mere economic calculating machines despite much of what modern economic theory says. We dislike losses more than we love profits to a mathematically illogical degree but during the internet bubble, many investors seemed to believe it was impossible to lose. Those investors became overconfident and interpolated historical returns too far into the futures just as Isaac did during the South Sea Company's enormous rally. The internet itself would increase the social aspect of investing as the coffeehouses near Exchange Alley did for speculators in 1720s. Even though nearly 280 years had passed, the biases remained unchanged. Only the names of the companies were new.

As the internet bubble inflated and new businesses were created, the narratives, and the people responsible for those narratives, often became more important than the economic prospects of the companies they founded. More than one academic has suggested that investors wanted to become players in the drama that was flowering and did so by using certain products and buying the shares of the company making them. But the stock market is often brimming with drama and personalities, so what made the internet bubble so special?

One difference is that aspects of this psychodrama were both external and internal. It was external in that investors saw the bubble inflating and allowed social dynamics and herding to pull them along, as Isaac was pulled along during the South Sea bubble and as millions of other investors have during other bubbles. But this episode was also intensely personal for many investors. They internalized their feelings about how the internet and its entrepreneurs could change them personally and make them feel special.

The external element of the drama reinforced salience bias, which is the tendency for investors to focus on noteworthy companies and to ignore others. This bias is strengthened by recency and vividness and the abundant press coverage increased the recency of attention of nearly anything that had to do with the internet while the novelty of it all heightened vividness. Professors Richard Taffler and David Tuckett have pointed out that when events are uncertain and ambiguous, which is always the case for investors, "it is emotions and states of mind which determine the way information and reality is apprehended." They note that as the press and word of mouth about the internet grew, "Such attention amplified exponentially the psychological desirability of owning internet stocks by exhibiting them so tantalizingly and so openly: they had all the characteristics required of phantastic [*sic*] objects—super, new, exhibitable [*sic*], not to mention enriching."

What made the internet bubble different and more dangerous is that these external cues were internalized as investors began trying to understand the internet and its impact on their identity, not just their finances. Taffler and Tuckett suggest how this happened: "The psychoanalytic approach to subjective experience concentrates on feelings as operating mentally separately from cognition. One may 'feel' one has 'it' while retaining perfectly clear cognitive capacities which, if salient, would allow one to see this is a gross exaggeration. In phantasy, by holding stock in internet firms, investors could unconsciously feel endowed with the actual qualities of the inventors, part of a magic circle of people 'in' on the new and possessing the mental equivalents of the primary phantastic objects of childhood."

This innovative technology seemed so powerful that it could transport people someplace new, and, in being transported, they felt they were omnipotent. More than with any bubble that came before it, what mattered was how investors *felt* about a potential company rather than the company's business model or balance sheet. These stocks and their larger-than-life founders took on an emotional aspect divorced from reality. Investors always get swept up by a stock market bubble, but this one was different because it wasn't merely a function of higher prices followed by still-higher prices; no, this bubble was accompanied by new technology that didn't exist when the bubble was in the price of tulip bulbs or housing. This emotional aspect had heretofore been reserved for sports heroes and movie stars, and just as those stars are able to transport us through imagination, the new internet companies were able to transport investors. After all, why would collectors pay thousands of dollars for a star baseball player's rookie baseball card if not to be transported back to a time when they were young, watching their hero take the field on a sunlit day, with the love of the game not yet tempered by the inability to hit a curveball or the intrusive realities of adulthood? The same sort of reverie was taking place among investors who dismissed concerns about profitability—if they considered them at all—and bought internet stocks because of how using a brand-new technology made them feel. These investors entered a financial fugue state.

This state was not something someone could "snap out of," because investors who are transported in this way are changed by the experience. In 1999, that change was often a willingness to approach stocks with radically new valuation methodologies because so many of these companies promised to change the world—some in small ways, some more profoundly—and investors wanted validation that would allow them to participate in the most intimate professional way possible: becoming "business partners" with their new heroes by buying their stock.

The problem for investors is that bubbles can't grow forever and as Tuckett and Taffler point out, the psychological stages of this infatuation follow a consistent psychological direction not unlike psychiatrist Elisabeth Kübler-Ross's five stages of grief. First, bullish investors experience fascination with whatever is new, followed by excitement, then euphoria. When the bubble inevitably bursts however, euphoria gives way to bargaining then panic which is followed by disgust, before the cycle ends in blame. Investors caught in the internet bubble were euphoric as 1999 ended.

As the Nasdaq Composite Index gained 85.6 percent that year, investors who had been transported relied on a roster of new, and nebulous, valuation metrics—just as some pamphleteers had done when trying to value the South Sea Company in 1720. Some internet analysts suggested that "engaged shopper" was the measure that mattered for websites trying to sell something, even though everyone had a different concept of what constituted an engaged shopper. Page views or unique monthly visitors became the metric preferred by Yahoo and other websites that weren't selling anything other than "eyeballs," another popular metric for sites that relied on advertising.

Some analysts even coined new words to justify the valuations for their favorite stocks. The term "mind share" barely existed in the English language before 1990 and its use ramped slowly as the decade progressed until investors clutched the concept as a rationale for buying internet stocks that might be relatively well known, or have substantial mind share, even if they produced little revenue and posted earnings that were less than zero.

The most perverted aspect of this new approach to stock market valuation was not that it ignored the sorts of measures that had been relied upon for centuries, but that it ridiculed those measures as not just irrelevant but dangerous. One analyst put it plainly, "Valuation is often not a helpful tool in determining when to sell hypergrowth stocks."

As the pamphleteers in 1720 had demonstrated, there are any number of ways to value a company, but before 1999 nearly every investor had agreed that the price-to-earnings ratio was relevant. What price was the stock trading at? How much profit, often called earnings, was the company making for each share of stock outstanding? The P/E ratio is the measure of how many years it will take for the company to pay for itself in the form of profits. If the ratio was very high, as it was for companies such as Yahoo, then investors expect them to increase profits. If a company wasn't generating any profit at all, like many internet stocks, then investors expected them to stop losing money and start making a bunch of it. Price-to-earnings ratio isn't infallible and is just one traditional metric for valuation, but as investors got carried away they disparaged traditional measures of valuation. The price-to-earnings ratio for the Nasdaq Composite Index had never exceeded 21 prior to 1995. In March 2000 it approached 100.

Investors should have asked themselves: if traditional measures of valuation weren't helpful, then what was? Eyeballs? Mind share? A warm, fuzzy feeling?

Some founders even thought profits were for suckers; they feared that if they generated a profit, investors would judge them insufficiently willing to burn through cash in a pell-mell effort to gain eyeballs or page views or mind share. But investors convinced themselves they were partners with the new internet celebrities and together they were going to change the world as long as they ignored issues as pedestrian as profitability, because it was different this time.

It is easy for investors to get carried away, or, as psychologists would say, transported, by exciting new companies. But while founders such as Jim Clark and Mark Andreessen may have thought they were on a mission, they always intended to make money eventually—they just didn't know how that was going to happen. Unfortunately for investors, this was a problem. The ones who got carried away would, as professional traders like to say, get carried out.

There have been several market bubbles and subsequent bear markets that were based on simple disagreement about the value of something without assuming it would change the world. The bubble in the price of tulip bulbs in the 1630s was all about price; nobody thought tulips would change the world. The bubble in South Sea shares was about price; although some investors were gulled into believing that trade with South America would prove immensely profitable, the nature of that trade was well understood. It was simply the frequency with which it would occur that was debated by a few.

The stock market bubble in the 1920s was largely about price although some of it was driven by new technologies that would indeed change the world. Automobiles had become widely available in the previous decade and automakers were a hot topic among investors. Another new technology was commercial radio, what many described as "music through the air," which blossomed in the 1920s. While only five commercial radio stations existed at the end of 1921, just six years later more than 680 crowded the airwaves as the amount of money spent on radios by American households increased by a factor of ten. Radio Corporation of America (RCA), was founded in 1919 and entered the 1920s with its stock trading on the "curb market"— literally a bunch of traders who gathered on the sidewalk outside the New York Stock Exchange to trade less important stocks. RCA closed 1921 at $2.25 a share only to reach a high of $570 in 1929.

While radio was a fascinating new technology, the Radio Corporation of America was just one of thirty stocks in the Dow Jones Industrial Average which was otherwise populated with old-line industrial firms such as American Tobacco, United States Rubber, F. W. Woolworth, and American Sugar Refining. Nobody thought these companies were going to change the world but they got bid up in price as the decade went on.

The stock market rally that ended abruptly in October 1987 was fueled by lower interest rates, increased corporate profits, and a resurgent confidence in America's place in the world, all of which made US companies more valuable. But it was not powered by the emergence of some transformative technology,

The internet bubble of the late 1990s was different. Indeed, perhaps the best comparison comes nearly two centuries prior, when investors were carried away in a transformational, personal manner. In 1830, the first commercial passenger railroad, the Liverpool and Manchester Railway, opened, linking the centers of Great Britain's industrial revolution. Soon other railroads were built and travelers were literally transported in a fashion they had thought impossible in the days when getting from one city to another was rare, as well as a dirty and laborious affair that relied on a horse-drawn coach. Coupled with the advances of the industrial revolution and the government sponsorship of railroad construction once the Liverpool and Manchester proved profitable, the British thought their world was being changed and expanded in a miraculous way. Those people who "got it" became investors and thousands of miles of additional railway were built. But when the Bank of England raised interest rates in late 1845, the flow of financing dried up and the bubble collapsed as reality intruded. Predictably, many of those who "got it" got taken in.

Investing is about making money. Because investors are human, they sometimes forget this and seek a different sort of sensation; that through their investments they are part of a movement that is more important than mere money. There are certainly things more important than money; millions of Americans, for instance, understandably refuse to invest in companies which produce tobacco products. But there's a flip side to that argument: a publicly traded company that aims to change the world may be worthy of your patronage, but that alone doesn't make it worthy of your investment.

The ethos that everything on the internet should be free was always going to be overwhelmed by the sheer amount of money that could be made. Jim Clark at Netscape didn't just want to make money, he *needed* to make money—and his competition wasn't going to make it easy for him. Bill Gates's Microsoft introduced its own Web browser, Internet Explorer, in 1995. It was free and came bundled with the dominant operating system of the time, Windows. For those new to browsers and the Web, using Microsoft's preinstalled browser was easier then downloading Navigator so that's what many did.

In the first objective sign that lots of money could be made from the internet (but that it wouldn't be easy, and the money wouldn't be limitless), in November 1998 Netscape agreed to sell itself to AOL for $4.2 billion. In another sign to investors, the price AOL paid was a slight discount to Netscape's valuation before the deal was announced.

The first internet businesses had the net at their core. They couldn't exist without it, and for the average user, these companies—including AOL, Netscape, and Yahoo—*were* the internet. But beginning in 1998 and then fully as 1999 dawned, a second wave of internet-centric businesses sprung up, using the internet to do what had been done before in person, by mail, or by phone. If it might be sold, someone thought it could be sold on the internet with companies being launched to sell pet supplies, handbags, short-subject movies, or restaurant recommendations. None of these founders imagined their companies would be profitable initially, and most had no clear path to profitability other than a Jim Clark–like confidence that the internet was going to be so big that it had to make everyone rich. Even the one aspect of the Web that had always cost money, actually connecting to it, gave way in 1998 when NetZero and other internet service providers began connecting users to the internet for free. As 1999 began, people could point to only two businesses that consistently made money via the Web: the *Wall Street*

Journal, which had gone online in 1996 and bucked the trend by charging a subscription fee from nearly its very first day, and purveyors of pornography. That was it. Investors should have paid attention.

Webvan was part of this second wave. Several sites, such as ShoeMall.com and Shoebuy.com, opened in an era when shoppers still expected to try on the shoes and walk around in them before purchasing. Kozmo.com was launched to sell and deliver most of what you could find at your neighborhood convenience store including candy, ice cream, fresh coffee, books, and VHS movie rentals. Kozmo.com would eventually raise more than $280 million in venture capital from partners including Amazon .com and Starbucks. All this came despite an admission from Kozmo's vice president in charge of international operations who told potential investors, "as it now exists, and one of the reasons it's suffering, is that it's not a whole lot different than a catalog model from fifty to a hundred years ago that Sears created in the United States." The company made a splash in February 2000 when it announced that it would pay Starbucks $150 million over the next five years. The coffeehouse chain would return $25 million of it as a venture capital investment but in exchange for the remaining $125 million it would allow Kozmo to place branded bins in Starbucks locations for returning those VHS rentals. Nothing Kozmo.com did in 1999 was magical, other than its penchant for summoning venture capitalists to appear with checks in hand.

Even companies that sold dog food and cat litter via the internet were red hot in 1999. Between January 1999 and March 2000, about one website a month was founded to peddle kibble, cat litter, and other pet supplies to the 60 percent of American households with pets. The market totaled $23 billion annually but was largely served by the brick-and-mortar chains PetSmart and Petco, both of which operated with the ruthless efficiency necessitated by miniscule profit margins of 2 percent to 2.5 percent typical on bulk products. But one web site had a sock puppet.

Pets.com was founded in August 1998 by serial entrepreneur Greg McLemore. As the internet bubble inflated, any good domain name coupled with a decent business concept was marketable and McLemore sold his embryonic Pets.com to venture capital firm Hummer Winblad early the next year. However, the business never made much sense. PetSmart and Petco were launching websites of their own and the additional competition from grocery stores and big-box retailers suggested that margins would only shrink further. That might have been fine; plenty of successful businesses operate with very low margins. But Pets.com was working on negative margins—for every dollar it paid product suppliers it collected just forty-three cents from customers. Pets.com's CEO, Julie Wainwright, called it "building ahead of the curve." And that was before it paid for overhead, shipping, salaries for its three hundred employees, and marketing—and Pets.com was spending *a lot* on marketing. From February to September 1999, Pets.com had total revenue of just $619,000 but spent $11.8 million on advertising. In November, it paid for its own float in the Macy's Thanksgiving Day Parade in New York City and on January 30, 2000, Pets.com joined the big time by spending $1.2 million on a thirty-second commercial during the Super Bowl.

The 2000 Super Bowl was like prom night for more than a

dozen nascent Web-based companies in a race to build "ahead of the curve" while establishing mind share and awareness if not profits and sustainable businesses. LifeMinders.com was created to collect intimate personal information from subscribers and send advertising-laced email reminders about anniversaries, birthdays, and the like. Its $1.2 million Super Bowl ad was little more than thirty seconds of a jarring neon-yellow background with black type that proclaimed, "This is the worst commercial on the Super Bowl." The graphic was paired with an atonal version of that staple of beginning piano students everywhere, "Chopsticks."

The unfortunately named Epidemic.com ran an ad showing a man getting paid for washing his hands in a public bathroom which was an odd juxtaposition for a company whose name gave no indication of what it did but rather described a widespread incidence of infectious disease, which started too often due to inadequate hand washing. The circular nature of the whole thing drowned out any marketing message. The company's national account manager would later admit, "The commercial drew little response from consumers . . ." but this confirmation of what everyone already knew came after the company had closed its doors while still owing its sixty employees their last paychecks.

Pets.com's $1.2 million bought it thirty off-key seconds filled with the company's sock puppet mascot mangling the band Chicago's pleading ballad "If You Leave Me Now." It was all an effort to get pet owners to order through its website and have purchases delivered rather than leave their pets at home even for a few moments. Through the traditional trappings of successful businesses—Super Bowl ads—it seemed as if these new kids on the internet block were trying to convince investors that there was nothing phantastic about their particular companies or the people running them. This approach could be productive only because there were other psychological quirks at work.

The recency effect is a phenomenon of memory in which the most recently encountered items are the most easily called to mind. It turns out that investors are more likely to buy shares in companies they've recently come across, regardless of the company's prospects, profits, or fundamental outlook. Isaac Newton had a small number of investment options in 1720, at least until the bubble companies were launched, but in 1999 there were more than 7,200 companies listed on US exchanges. It would have been easy for Isaac to list all the joint-stock companies available for him to invest in. In 1999 it would have require an impressive feat of memory to call to mind a tiny fraction of the listed companies, so modern investors tend to focus on the stocks they have encountered most recently.

This tendency dramatically reduces the range of investment options available to the average investor who has a finite amount of attention and thus tends to buy stocks that stand out for whatever reason. Ask yourself, how many stocks in the S&P 500 index, the most important equity index in American finance, you can name? How could you consider investing in any stock in the S&P 500 that you can't call to mind? Those stocks might as well not exist at all. What about the other 3,500 or so publicly traded companies in the United States?

If we can call to mind only a small fraction of the publicly traded companies in the United States, how do the companies we actually invest in come to our attention in the first place? Often an investor has heard about a particular stock simply because it has recently had a big move in price or has experienced much higher than average trading volume. Either factor would be noteworthy, but neither necessarily recommends a company as a long-term investment. Maybe the company is mentioned frequently in the media because it has a charismatic but not very effective CEO? Or maybe the company is in the news because it was the subject of a "pump-and-dump" scheme on the part of a twenty-three-year-old pharmacy student and his friend.

Recency bias generates poorer investment returns in several ways. One is by undermining attempts at diversification. Reducing the size of the investible universe through recency and salience results in a portfolio that is less diversified than it should be despite diversification's undeniable benefits. Portfolios subject to recency and salience also overweight the stocks of companies that are physically located near the investor, even though diversification away from companies headquartered nearby would have particular advantages if those companies faced hard times and laid off a substantial portion of the headquarters staff, depressing the local economy. Finally, they result in investors holding too much stock of companies in the industry in which they are employed even though diversification to other industries would, again, have advantages if the industry an investor works in faces tough times. The last thing an investor needs is to lose his job and simultaneously have his portfolio fare particularly poorly because he invested disproportionately in companies from that industry.

Recency bias also undermines returns by leading investors to believe that recent performance, that which is most easily called to mind, will continue into the future without regard to longer-term trends or the base case. That tendency led Isaac Newton to buy back into South Sea Company stock near the top, confident that it would continue its amazing advance even though the longer-term trend, the base case, was that South Sea stock was worth about £100 a share. In a related quirk, recency bias leads investors to throw in the towel and sell at the bottom because they think a downward trend will continue and their loss aversion kicks in.

Availability bias is closely related to recency and salience. Availability bias is the tendency to use easily recalled memories to estimate the probability of some event happening. Often these memories are dramatic, and thus not representative of everyday events. The more readily something comes to mind, the higher our estimate of the probability of it occurring. For example, individuals who had an acquaintance recently go through a divorce give higher estimates of the general incidence of divorce in a population. Something similar is true for recent victims of crime. And we tend to overestimate the likelihood of the most dramatic causes of death, such as murder (19,454 homicides were reported in 2017) and underestimate unremarkable causes of death such as chronic lower respiratory disease (which claimed 160,201 lives that year).

Similarly, it is easy to recall any stock market crash you've lived through and name many others that you didn't personally experience. Availability skews our perceptions of the likelihood of stock market crashes, which has real consequences for investors. Except for those who are overconfident and believe the rare is impossible, many investors tend to deploy money as if another crash is much more likely than it actually is, and their returns suffer. Consequently, they worry too much about a stock market crash on the order of 1929 or 1987 and adjust their holdings accordingly but don't worry enough about starting to save early, or assuming an amount of risk appropriate for their age, or the size of the fees charged on their investments. Why do we pay more attention to the sensational and less, or none, to the ordinary? Much of it has to do with the emotions generated by extraordinary events.

As business professor Eric Johnson and the Nobel Prize–winning psychologist Amos Tversky pointed out in 1983, "One characteristic that distinguishes judgments about risks from other estimates . . . is that they seldom occur in an emotionally neutral context. When we witness an accident or read a newspaper report about a natural disaster, we do not merely revise our subjective probabilities [give in to availability bias]; we are also shaken and disturbed."

Johnson and Tversky went on to conduct an experiment that manipulated mood, which they called "affect," by having a test subject read a brief news account of a tragic event. This "priming" of the subject's mood generated an increase in his or her estimate of the likelihood of a number of risks and undesirable events, many of which had nothing to do with the news account just read. For example, reading about a student who had succumbed to leukemia led the subjects to increase their estimate of the likelihood of dying from an airplane crash or lightning strike. Oddly, priming the subject's mood with a positive, uplifting story didn't have a commensurate impact. This effect works only in one direction.

Think for a moment about how hearing that the stock market lost 5 percent today might impact your decision-making. Now think about how you might react to learning that the stock market gained 5 percent today. The manifest danger is that any news that might "prime" your emotions is likely to drive – our word 'emotion' comes from the Latin root which means 'drive' - investment decisions today. The impact of today's decision will compound over the next thirty years, even though the news that started the whole cascade of emotions and consequences is almost certain to be irrelevant thirty years from now.

For too long, we assumed investors were like computers, saving the right amount each month and investing that money only after a rigorous analysis of risks, potential rewards, portfolio construction, and time frame for all the investments available, not just the ones they can recall. We've failed to recognize and, more importantly, teach investors about the impact of emotions on investing. And when we do, we focus on how we will feel when the results are known rather than identifying the emotions that are at work when we make the original investment decision. Paul Samuelson's risk-averse colleague who refused the coin-flipping bet even though the odds were on his side didn't want to wager because of the emotions he believed he might experience *after* the coin had been flipped. Researchers call these anticipated emotions. To the degree that investors allow anticipated emotions to overwhelm making smart investment choices now, they're destructive. The young investor who refuses to put even a portion of her retirement savings in stocks because she knows she would hate to learn that the value of her portfolio has declined is allowing anticipated emotions to drive investment decisions that are clearly misguided.

One essential way that anxious investors can improve their long-term outcome is to try not to speculate on how they might feel looking back after decades of investing. Rather, you should practice a sort of financial mindfulness, disciplining yourself to make logical investment decisions now despite the knowledge that they might not always work out. The economist who wouldn't risk $100 to win $200 could have taken this approach.

To outwit the emotions we feel at the moment we must decide whether to make a wager or investment, we must first understand them. Researchers call these anticipatory emotions; they are important because if an investor makes better decisions now—decisions that recognize the impact of our mood as we're making them—it is much less likely that he or she will let fear take charge in the heat of the moment and sell out at the bottom of a bear market. It's also less likely that they will focus on only those companies which appear most frequently in the news, or had eye-popping results last year, or are headquartered nearby, or operate in the industry in which they work.

The proper approach can be helpful because risk-as-feeling generates poorer choices than the purely objective calculus of payoffs and probabilities investors have been assumed to adopt. Some have learned this about us and know how to take advantage of it—no group more so than the insurance industry. Purchasing insurance should be an objective decision based on the potential loss, its likelihood, the cost of the insurance, and the buyer's wealth and risk tolerance. But those selling insurance have learned that "images of losses that evoke vivid negative mental imagery" tend to sell more insurance. For instance, one research study showed that air travelers were willing to pay more for travel insurance that paid out only in the event of a death caused by "terrorist acts" —an extremely vivid circumstance—than they were willing to pay for insurance that covered death from "all possible causes," which would have *included* terrorist acts as well as other, more prosaic, causes lacking such vividness.

This sort of market inefficiency—paying more for insurance against a specific cause of death than for insurance against any cause of death—is a result of risk-as-feeling and was evident among internet investors in early 2000.

The Palm Pilot was the first popular handheld computer. It included an electronic calendar, address book, notepad, and other productivity functions in a package about the size of a modern smartphone. Information was entered on the screen using a stylus and an ingenious handwriting recognition system. Palm, the company that made the Pilot, wasn't of the Web but had captured the phantastic zeitgeist of the internet era and in 1999 it controlled 70 percent of the market for what had become known as personal digital assistants.

Palm was a division of 3Com, an old-line maker of the technology at the heart of the internet including data switches, controllers, and routers. But 3Com wasn't well known except by those few who were aware it owned the company that made the fascinating Palm Pilot. Recency and salience were working against 3Com and many who did know about the two companies became convinced that Palm would be better off on its own, free to target its marketing to individual consumers who were a mystery to 3Com. So, in September 1999, 3Com announced that it would spin off its ownership of Palm.

Palm had its initial public offering on March 2, 2000 with 3Com selling 5 percent of its stake. 3Com planned to divest its remaining shares over the next few months by distributing 1.525 shares of Palm to 3Com shareholders for each share of 3Com they held. The owner of 100 shares of 3Com would still own 100 shares of 3Com but would also own 152.5 shares of Palm once the spinoff was complete. This arrangement made the math easy; each share of 3Com should be worth at least one and a half times that of each Palm share, and since 3Com had $10 of cash in the bank per share as well as its profitable legacy business of supplying communications equipment to corporate users, its stock should have cost even more than that. Precisely how much more would depend on how one valued 3Com's remaining business and while that value was open for debate, it should be substantial since 3Com was the second largest player in the space, trailing only Cisco.

Palm closed at $95.06 a share on its first day of trading. That meant that 3Com, with its remaining stake in Palm, $10 in cash per share, and its legacy business, should have been worth at least $155 per share and likely much more. Instead, 3Com closed at $81.81 a share, a decline of 21 percent for the day. People who purchased one share of Palm at $95.06 could have had 1.525 shares for a total of just $81.81 by buying a share of 3Com instead. The stock market was, in essence, saying that 3Com's profitable legacy business was worth negative $63 a share. These weren't the only illogical decisions investors would make as they gave way to their biases and quirks.

ComputerLiteracy.com doesn't seem too tough a domain name to spell correctly, particularly for a site that was, according to the company, aimed at readers with "large intellects." But in March 1999 the online seller of technical books and manuals decided to make a name change to eliminate any risk of misspellings which might lead potential customers astray. Executives decided that FatBrain.com was the answer to their problems. On the day the news of the name change hit the market, the company's stock rallied by 33 percent.

Many other business leaders thought a name change would similarly help their stock price, and while the newly renamed FatBrain.com had always been in the computer and internet space, some thought that bump in stock price might be available even if their company had nothing to do with the internet. Between June 1, 1998, and July 31, 1999, ninety-five publicly traded companies changed their corporate names to some sort of internet-related "dot com" or "dot-net" name. Many of these companies had nothing to do with the internet before their rechristening, and some planned not to change at all on that score. New name, but same old business plan.

One example was Windom Inc., a shell company that had been founded in 1988 but had no assets or business operations from the moment it was incorporated until 1997. In August 1991, a substantial percentage of Windom's outstanding shares were distributed to plaintiffs and plaintiffs' attorneys as a result of a class-action lawsuit against its parent. In 1997, Windom merged with the New York Bagel Exchange, a company whose entire business amounted to a single delicatessen. Two years later, all the bagel and restaurant operations were sold for just $120,000, leaving the New York Bagel Exchange a corporate shell with no ongoing business—not even that one lonely deli. At that point, the company changed its name to WebBoat.com and, finally, it seems it had found success. Four days before the name change, New York Bagel Exchange shares were trading at $5. Four days after the company adopted its new name they were trading at $8.75, a gain of 75 percent.

That jump in price turned out to be about average. Of the ninety-five stocks that announced name changes during that period, the average gain for the ten days surrounding the announcement was 74 percent. And despite the questionable logic of investors buying these stocks merely because of a name change, the effect didn't fade. As researchers wrote in 2001, "A mere association with the internet seems enough to provide a firm with a large and permanent value increase."

The only semi-logical explanation is a behavioral one; investors were caught up in a mania which focused on internet stocks in an orgy of recency and phantastical thinking. There was a belief that how one "felt" about a stock was more important than its prospects. As prices continued higher the phantasies became self-fulfilling as more investors became emotional about internet stocks and bought them, driving prices even higher. Professor Robert Shiller calls this a naturally occurring

Ponzi process, and, like the illegal one, it requires new people to sustain higher prices. When the supply of new money fizzles out, the result is always the same. The job of today's anxious investor is to not get caught up in the frenzy.

The orgy didn't stop. The Nasdaq Composite Index gained 22 percent in December 1999 and another 19 percent in February 2000. Both monthly performances significantly exceeded the average *annual* return since the index had been created in 1971. The Nasdaq hit another all-time high on March 10, 2000. After gaining 85.6 percent in 1999, the index had grown by another 24.1 percent so far in 2000 and, at that rate, would more than double by the end of the year. The closing high of 5,048.62 on March 10, 2000 was the forty-ninth all-time high in the previous hundred trading days as investors grew overconfident that the previous year's trend would continue even though it was clearly preposterous. The high on March 10 would also be the top.

Some of the big names, including Yahoo, AOL, and NetZero, had shown warning signs months before. When the Nasdaq peaked on March 10, Yahoo was 25.3 percent below its fifty-two-week high; AOL, 32.8 percent below its fifty-two-week high; and NetZero, the company trying to put AOL out of business by giving away the internet for free, was 41.9 percent below its fifty-two-week high. Amazon was still selling just books, but of all the sites selling something, Jeff Bezos's brainchild was the quintessence. It was also a relative old-timer, having gone public nearly three years earlier, and its losses were in line with the companies that were now part of the internet. On March 10 it closed at $66.88, 40.8 percent below its highest level from the previous December.

Many investors had finally come to realize that valuations for these companies—at least, old-style valuations, such as the price-to-earnings ratio, which focused on traditional measures like profitability—were impossible to rationalize given current share prices. Some of this was due to the epiphany that while so many new sites had opened to sell stuff, traditional retailers weren't simply going to roll over and let websites take their business. For instance, the popular clothing chain the Gap had gone online in 1997. While Macys.com had started as a purely informational site in 1996, it was relaunched two years later as a full-on sales outlet. Similarly, in late 1999, Walmart's website was reworked to make the largest retailer in the country a presence in e-commerce. PetSmart and Petco had websites to compete with the hapless Pets.com. Booksellers like Borders and Barnes and Noble had started their own websites to compete with Amazon.

Unfortunately, that competition cut in both directions. For example, Amazon didn't have a monopoly on selling books on the internet but it was one of the businesses whose shareholders didn't care that it was losing money—in fact, some Amazon shareholders preferred that the company lose money in its race for market share. Accordingly, on May 17, 1999, Amazon announced it would cut the price of best-selling books by 50 percent. Barnesandnoble.com and Borders.com matched the price cuts within hours. The *New York Times* reported that halving prices would cause all three to "almost certainly lose money on the bargain sales." Investors thought of the newly priced best sellers as loss leaders— like a grocery store marking down the price of milk or bread to get customers into the store. But grocery shoppers buy dozens of items, making up for the store's loss on any single item, while the latest best seller is often the only book people buy. At this rate, the march toward profitability for internet retailers now seemed much more arduous and uncertain than it had when the sheer scale of the opportunity seemed to guarantee profitability.

By March 2000 the bubble had already burst—the market just didn't know it yet. It was the newest names—the ones that had just gone public and had more tenuous connections to the internet—that were driving a last gasp as investors were certain someone would come along to pay even more for their shares. Webvan had gone public in November 1999. Fogdog, an online sporting goods retailer, went public in December at $11 a share, giving it a market capitalization of $468 million despite having total revenue of less than $3 million in the four months prior to its IPO. Neoforma.com combined two businesses: selling medical equipment and supplies to health care providers, a business that already had a large and formidable group of old-line competitors, and an auction business similar to eBay albeit for used medical equipment. The company went public on January 24, 2000 at $13 a share. It closed the first day at $52.38, a gain of more than 300 percent giving Neoforma.com a total market capitalization of nearly $3 billion even though it had total revenue of just $460,000 in the two months prior to and after its IPO. Other businesses had done all of this long before the World Wide Web even existed.

March 10, the day the Nasdaq Composite made its all-time high, was a Friday and there was no extraordinary news that weekend. Nonetheless, the Nasdaq Composite Index opened 3.4 percent lower on Monday. It rallied a bit from there and it would have been easy to think that morning's downward blip was a missed buying opportunity. There hadn't been many dips over the past few years and as the index spent the day gaining back much of its opening loss, some were kicking themselves for not taking advantage. The dumbest internet companies had wasted a bunch of money on those stupid Super Bowl ads but many of the others promised to change the world. Some seemed like they really might. The year 2000 was the first that had a majority of Americans using the internet, thanks in large part to AOL and Yahoo, and the internet was certainly changing a few lives if it was not yet changing the broader world.

Some of the companies were changing too. AOL had announced on January 10, 2000, that it would buy Time Warner, the owner of the iconic Warner Brothers movie studio, cable TV powerhouse CNN, and *Time* magazine, for $182 billion in stock. *Time* had introduced Marc Andreesen to America when it put him on its cover and called him one of the "Golden Geeks" in 1996. Now the venerable news magazine and the rest of Time Warner was being bought by one. Amazon's revenue had more than doubled to over $1.6 billion in 1999. Yahoo had revenue of $592 million, more than double its figure from the previous year, and net profit of $48 million— impressive results compared to their year-earlier loss of $15 million and very impressive compared to all the other internet companies that couldn't make money at all. It was those other companies that were the problem. The Nasdaq started the week by losing 2.8 percent on Monday, 4.1 percent on Tuesday, and 2.6 percent on Wednesday, but it rebounded on Thursday and Friday and fell by just 5 percent for the week. Then it really started.

The anxious investor will receive two seemingly conflicting pieces of advice. The first is to stay invested, avoiding both loss aversion (the urge to sell at the bottom) and disposition (the impulse to sell winners). The other is to be disciplined, which would seem to suggest not being greedy and "taking money off the table" when prices are high. But that's the wrong definition of discipline for investors. Being disciplined means not assuming you can time the market but instead understanding the behavioral quirks and biases that can sabotage our investment returns, and then building a reasonable portfolio that doesn't own stocks merely because they're phantastic or salient. Being disciplined entails sticking with that plan and portfolio and continuing to fund investment accounts even when things seem ugly.

Over the weekend of Sunday, March 19, *Barron's*, the weekly newspaper focused on investing, published a story by Jack Willoughby about the amount of cash many internet companies were burning through. The very first sentence asked, "When will the internet Bubble burst?" Not *if*, but *when* Willoughby then vivisected the publicly traded internet companies, detailing how "scores" of them would fail by the end of the year as they ran out of cash because they had "little realistic hope of profits in the near term." He detailed how the avenues for raising more capital were being cut off for the 74 percent of the 207 internet companies with negative cash flow that his article examined. He then explained the likely damage, given that "several signs suggest that the era of 'unglued' stock prices is fast approaching" and how "Investors' distaste for 'Net stocks is especially prevalent" when the business focused on selling to consumers. He used the grocery delivery service Peapod, a rival of Webvan with the same problems, as an example. Peapod wasn't profitable and it was losing so much money so quickly that with just $3 million in cash, its "coffers could be empty within a month."

The article was well reasoned and supported by data. It was also damning and the sort of wake-up call that could jar investors who were paying more attention to 1999's 85.6 percent gain in the Nasdaq Composite than the 11.9 percent annualized gain it returned from 1972 to 1995, or the combined loss of 55.3 percent the index suffered in 1973 and 1974. It reminded investors that the way they *felt* about a particular risk couldn't substitute for trying to objectively analyze the risk. And it likely reminded investors that no matter how much long-distance affection they might have felt for some of these entrepreneurs, they weren't friends or buddies or business partners.

When trading opened on Monday, March 20, the profitable internet companies such as Yahoo and AOL gained ground. But the broader market was made up of companies that weren't profitable, and so, while Webvan lost 7.9 percent that day and NetZero fell 14.7 percent and FogDog, dropped 10.9 percent, the Nasdaq Composite Index dipped 3.9 percent.

The Nasdaq Composite ended March at 4,572.83, a loss of just 2.6 percent from the end of February. While the loss pushed the index nearly 10 percent below its March 10 all-time high, that sort of volatility was common given how the market had performed during the previous December and February and how ominous *Barron's* magazine's predictions had seemed.

With so much at stake, it was just a matter of time before companies were accused of wrongdoing. The same US government that would later indict Hootan Melamed and Arash Aziz-Golshani for stealing $364,000 by manipulating the price of Webworld stock, decided to start with the largest of them. In May 1998, the US Department of Justice and twenty states sued Microsoft, charging that Bill Gates's behemoth had abused its power as the dominant provider of computer operating systems by forcing computer manufacturers to include its Internet Explorer on new computers with the goal of crippling Netscape. Even though Netscape eventually sold itself to AOL, the Microsoft case continued to march through the courts.

On Friday, November 5, 1999, Judge Thomas Penfield Jackson ruled that Microsoft had indeed abused its monopoly power and "demonstrated that it will use its prodigious market power and immense profits to harm any firm that insists on pursuing initiatives that could intensify competition against one of Microsoft's core products." John D. Rockefeller's Standard Oil was broken up in 1911 into thirty-three different companies because of antitrust concerns that sprang from his anticompetitive activities. A similar fate seemed to await Microsoft as 1999 ended, an outcome so potentially draconian that the company appealed immediately—even before Jackson had made a final ruling or levied any penalty.

Judge Jackson had been unstinting when crafting his initial

decision but he also realized that breaking up Microsoft would take years and be immensely complicated, both legally and technologically. It would also have other far-reaching and unintended consequences, so on November 19 he ordered the two sides into mediation to reach a "voluntary settlement." Despite this opportunity to negotiate a solution, things had not improved for Microsoft by the end of March 2000. News broke that Gates had been embarrassed in a number of depositions and that some who witnessed one of them called him "evasive and nonresponsive." *BusinessWeek* would report that a particular performance by the Microsoft cofounder and CEO was so incredulous that the judge laughed out loud when the video was played in court.

Late on Friday, March 24, 2000, Microsoft made its final settlement proposal and agreed to separate Internet Explorer from the Windows operating system. Given that Microsoft's browser had now eclipsed Navigator in number of users, as well as the fact that Netscape had been forced into the arms of AOL, the government believed Microsoft, having gotten what it wanted, expected to rob the bank and keep the loot. Government lawyers were confident in their case; Judge Jackson's initial ruling that Microsoft had abused its market power—he had called it a "finding of fact"—meant they had the upper hand. Over the weekend, and just seven days after Jack Willoughby's damning story in *Barron's* had detailed the dangers for investors, reports surfaced that the government considered Microsoft's offer "inadequate." Come Monday, Microsoft opened down 3.5 percent and only tumbled further from there, losing

6.8 percent by the time markets closed. The Nasdaq lost 7.9 percent that week.

Things got worse the next weekend when newspapers reported that another judge who had been appointed to lead mediation efforts between the government and Microsoft thought "the disagreements among the parties . . . are too deep-seated to be bridged" and was ending his attempts to negotiate a settlement. All that was left now was for Judge Jackson to deliver his verdict that Microsoft had indeed violated antitrust laws and announce the penalty. Microsoft opened 11.1 percent lower on Monday, April 3, and ended the day down 14.5 percent. The Nasdaq Composite lost 7.6 percent. It was already more than 16 percent below its recent high.

April 2000 was a horrible month. Investors began to realize that while pure internet stocks were the ones infected, the biggest technology names were going to get sick too, just as Jack Willoughby had warned in *Barron's*. On April 8, 2000, the *Economist* magazine published an article about internet stocks in its "Monopoly Money" column and asked, "How low can it go?" The piece pointed out that the price-to-earnings ratio for the Nasdaq Composite Index was 62, meaning that an investor paid $62 for each $1 of profit generated annually by all the companies in the index. Prior to 1995, the ratio had "never exceeded 21." By this standard, stock prices were nearly triple what they should have been.

The Nasdaq Composite entered a bear market on April 12 when it lost more than 7 percent and closed more than 25 percent below the high made barely a month earlier. The index ultimately lost 15.6 percent in April, its fifth worst month ever to that point. Intel, maker of most of the computer chips at the heart of personal computers, lost 3.9 percent that month. Cisco, maker of the networking hardware that ran the internet, lost 10.3 percent just one month after it had become the most valuable US company.

Yahoo Stock Price, April 1996 - December 2004

Then the Nasdaq Composite lost 11.9 percent in May, ending the month 32.6 percent below its high. Some of the stocks making up the index were much worse off; Yahoo was down by 52.4 percent and Amazon was down 54.7 percent. The latest group of companies to conduct IPOs, the ones that merely used the internet to sell stuff, were performing even worse: Webvan was down by 80.3 percent; Pets.com, which had gone public just seventy-six days earlier, had already lost 81.0 percent; and Fogdog was down 83.5 percent.

What do investors do when their phantasy stocks become nightmares? In the spring and summer of 2000, some investors cycled from euphoria to fear to panic, while others had taken the next step to disgust. Soon they were also turning against everyone and everything they had believed in so stridently just a few months before in the final step in the cycle, assigning blame.

Revulsion and finger-pointing in the wake of a market collapse is not new. The British Parliament started an investigation into the South Sea Company debacle to fix blame and arrested the directors of the company lest convenient scapegoats flee. Ultimately, the chancellor of the exchequer and several members of Parliament were blamed and expelled from office. Since the epic stock market crash of 1907, nearly every modern economic disaster or stock market crash has been followed by the creation of a government agency or appointment of a government commission and the release of a big, thick, square book chronicling findings and assigning blame. The Securities and Exchange Commission was created after the crash of 1929 to assure that finger pointing in subsequent crashes had the force of law.

Even in a savage bear market like the one going on in April and May 2000, there is a logical course of action for every investor. While timing the market effectively is impossible, harvesting losses will reduce or postpone taxes. In tax-loss harvesting, an investor sells an investment at a loss which offsets gains realized when other investments are sold at a profit. The amount of loss that can be deducted against other types of income is limited and an investor has to wait thirty days to buy back the same investment—or a "substantially identical" one—but tax-loss harvesting offers undeniable benefits.

Making certain a portfolio is still properly diversified will reduce risk without reducing return. It is productive to review both how you arrived at past investment decisions and how stocks you unloaded performed afterward.

Kübler-Ross's third stage of grief is "bargaining," and investors were doing that now. Another word for what they were doing is hoping. The two have the same impact on stock performance: none. Many traders and investors have uttered the "Trader's Prayer" which goes, "Please God, just get me back to even and I'll get out." This is anchoring and it has likely cost more traders more money than any other behavioral quirk.

Anchoring is the tendency to rely too much on the first piece of information or the most salient piece of information when making a decision, without regard to its relevance. For many investors in the summer of 2000, the anchor price for the internet stocks they owned was the price they had paid originally, even if the stock was now trading substantially lower. That anchor price wasn't any legitimate measure of the stock's present value; its present value was whatever price it was trading at. An investor's entry price is no more important than the winning numbers from those previous spins of the roulette wheel that casinos post for gamblers to see.

This was far from the first time investors, even professionals, were led astray by anchoring. In the responses to Robert

Shiller's survey following the 1987 crash, 37 percent of institutional investors said they expected a recovery because prices had fallen "too far too fast." Why would these professional investors believe last week's prices were a better measure of value than this week's prices? This is quintessential anchoring. Some of the respondents did reference long-term value but less than 14 percent of them said they expected a rebound because of low prices themselves.

To demonstrate the impact of anchoring, famed behavioral psychologists Amos Tversky and Daniel Kahneman had test subjects observe an experimenter spin a wheel that had the numbers from 0 through 100. The experimenter then had the test subject move up or down from the number the wheel had landed on until they arrived at their estimation of the percentage of countries in the United Nations which are in Africa. Clearly their starting point—the random number that the wheel landed on—has no impact on the right answer but for those who saw the wheel stop on 10, the median answer to the question of the percentage of countries in the United Nations from Africa was 25 percent. For those who saw the wheel stop on 65, the median answer was 45 percent. The number the test subjects started from was their anchor and it had a significant impact on their guesses, though there was clearly no relation between the two. (As of 2021, there were 193 member states in the United Nations and 54 of them, or 28 percent, belonged to the African Group.)

The same anchoring was going on among investors who owned internet stocks in the spring of 2000. Their entry price was the anchor price similar to the number Tversky and Kahneman's wheel had stopped on. Investors watched as the price moved down from that anchor price but their estimation of the value of each share of stock was impacted by their starting point. Especially for those who had bought at the very top, their estimation of value was much higher than the current market price.

This adoption of their entry price as an anchor price and investors' bargaining with the market seemed to be working as spring gave way to summer. The Nasdaq Composite Index gained nearly 17 percent in June, lost a mere 5 percent in August, and rose just over 11 percent in September. It was back above 4,200 and no longer technically in a bear market. Those who wanted a little bit more, or needed a little bit more to have their prayer answered, believed the broader market was now on their side and headed in the right direction.

But internet stocks weren't participating as the rest of the market rallied. While the index had done so well since the end of May, Yahoo lost another 19.5 percent, AOL gained less than 1 percent, Webvan fell another 54 percent, and NetZero lost another 73 percent. As for Pets.com, the company's stock was trading for just 75 cents a share. It had traded more than 17 million shares and was above $9 a share in March but in September it traded a little more than 2.3 million shares so it wasn't even attractive to the attention-seeking denizens of the over-the-counter bulletin board who normally loved to throw around dollar-cheap stocks. All the Kübler-Ross bargaining with the market wasn't going to spare internet stocks.

Investors might ask if this bounce doesn't prove that the anchoring-induced refusal to sell losers is a good thing if we can't time the market. Isn't this sort of waiting good if it keeps an investor from selling at the bottom? The mental process might be tortured, but isn't the outcome ultimately positive? No. First, this sort of anchoring distorts an investor's view of value and makes it more difficult to make rational decisions. Second, attention is a finite resource so anything that consumes it without benefit is a waste. Finally, there are things to be done and this mental running in place prevents an investor from taking the best action. Nearly every investor who owned Pets. com had an unrealized loss and investors who didn't harvest tax losses were making a mistake. Other investors were making a different mistake by telling themselves to hang on, believing it couldn't get much worse. Actually, it could get worse. It could get 75 cents worse. This thinking exemplifies the disposition effect at its extreme and by the end of October, Pets.com had tumbled another 33 percent to just 50 cents a share.

Investors are craziest when they're losing money and they were losing lots of it as the brief summer rally gave way to more downside. The Nasdaq lost 12.7 percent in September, 8 percent in October, and nearly 23 percent in November. While some were hanging on, others were selling. Those hanging on and refusing to sell their losers had become like the bettors at the racetrack who become risk seeking and wager all they have left on the longest shot in the last race.

Investors tend to become risk averse when they have a gain and will choose to realize the sure gain while forgoing the possibility of an even larger gain. When they suffer a loss, they become risk seeking and will forego a sure loss while taking the risk of a larger loss if it offers the potential for getting back to even, which is what so many investors were praying for. This is the heart of the disposition effect.

Tversky and Kahneman called these competing tendencies prospect theory because they compare human responses to a certain prospect and a risky prospect. They demonstrated the absurdity of these different, but intensely human, tendencies by asking students and faculty a series of hypothetical questions which focused on decision-making under risk.

First, study participants were asked to choose between (a) a guaranteed 3,000 units of a currency or (b) a wager that had an 80 percent chance of returning 4,000 units and a 20 percent chance of returning zero. The mathematical "expected value" of this second alternative is 3,200 units, more than the value of the first option. Yet four out of five subjects chose the certain, less valuable option. People are risk averse in the gain domain. They tend to sell winners.

But when subjects were asked if they would prefer a certain loss of 3,000 units or accept a wager that had an 80 percent chance of a 4,000-unit loss with a 20 percent chance of zero loss, they chose the second option even though it was mathematically inferior. People are risk seeking in the loss domain. They tend to hold on to losers.

Investors in internet companies in the autumn of 2000 were operating in the loss domain so they were risk seeking. Holding on to Pets.com at 75 cents is understandable, if not wise, in this situation. The best investors refuse to fall prey to this tendency.

While some investors were afraid, some companies were afraid as well. They feared that the general disdain of any internet-related investment in the last months of 2000 would pull down their share price, regardless of the fundamental value of their business. They had enjoyed the ride when this association was pushing prices higher but wanted to get off now that it had swung in the other direction. So, just as some companies in previous years had added *.com* or *.net* to their names even if the nature of the business didn't change, after the bubble burst, some managers removed *.com* from their companies' names. Five university researchers followed the sixty-one publicly traded companies that changed their names after February 2000 from something internet specific to something more neutral. Their share price performance in the period that began thirty days before the name change was announced and ended thirty days later was 64 percentage points better than that of an index made up of internet stocks.

In an Associated Press article about the phenomenon, one observer remarked, "Companies are distancing themselves from that smell." No business name could be more of the internet than Internet.com, and it took the round-trip. In 1998, Mecklermedia was a publisher of magazines and websites focused on the business of the internet so the company changed its name to Internet.com. But it would change it again in 2001 to the purposefully enigmatic INTMedia Group in order to avoid the stench. Company CEO and founder Alan Meckler was frank about the reason for the second change, saying, "It's window dressing for the financial community. For those in the know, our customers, nothing ever changed." Again it seemed important to "get it," to be "in the know."

The reverse name changes were the clearest sign that internet stocks were reviled. It wasn't just internet stocks that were out of favor as 2000 came to an end. On December 5, the British tabloid the *Daily Mail* declared, "Internet 'May Be Just a Passing Fad as Millions Give Up on It.'" The article described how "millions were turning their back on the World Wide Web" because of its limitations and the cost of connecting. It referenced a study claiming that email wasn't replacing other means of communication but was merely contributing to information overload. And for those interested less in the broad impact of the internet and more in the impact on internet stocks, the study said, "the future of online shopping is limited." It went on to suggest some users were bored while others were frustrated. Certainly some were dismayed by the internet if investing in its stocks had cost so many so much money and if the only businesses that found it consistently profitable were the *Wall Street Journal* and a bunch of pornographers.

The Nasdaq Composite Index closed out 2000 at 2,470.52. That was a 39.3 percent loss for the year but a 51.1 percent loss from the peak made on March 10. The index would continue to drop and would take another leg down, along with the rest of our stock market, following September 11, 2001. Just as it took Isaac Newton some time to come to grips with his losses, investors took some time to realize that Webvan and Pets.com weren't worthy of being their phantasy stocks. Self-discovery takes longer than we'd like.

In October 2000, Fogdog.com, the online sporting goods retailer, was acquired by another on-line sporting goods retailer for just $38.4 million. By the time the deal was consummated in December 2000, Fogdog stock had dropped from a high of $22 to just 50 cents a share in less than thirteen months. In November 2000, Pets.com ceased operations and in January 2001 it liquidated its few remaining assets. Its last day as a public company was January 18, 2001 and the stock closed at 12.5 cents a share. Webvan declared bankruptcy in June 2001. Its last day trading as a public company was July 6, 2001 when the stock closed at 6 cents. It had survived for more than a year and a half as a public company, enough time to lose $830 million.

Webvan Stock Price, November 1999 - July 2001

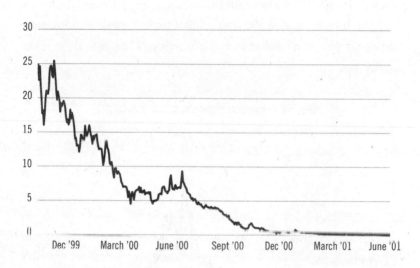

Investors do as much damage to themselves during bubbles as they do during crashes. It is so easy to think it is indeed different this time, just as investors in British railroads in the 1830s had thought everything was different. It rarely is for travelers or for users of the internet and it never is for investors.

It is natural for investors to be captivated by the next new thing. They look back at the same old things that were once the next new things and wish they had loaded up on Microsoft in 1986 or Amazon in 2001 or Google in 2004 or Apple in 2007 when it introduced the iPhone. Hindsight bias tells us we should be able to identify the next hot stock but we're wrong. We forget that by June 2001, Palm was trading at just $6.50 a share and that the company would be acquired outright in 2010 for $5.70 a share. We forget about all the other highfliers that fell to earth because we never hear about them, outside of a snide joke, so they're not salient.

We fool ourselves. We don't mean to, but we do. And sometimes we just can't recognize the danger. That would be true again too.

Nasdaq Composite Index, 1995 - 2003

Irrationality

You would think that at least one of the behavioral biases would work to an investor's benefit. But as we discovered in the previous chapter, although disposition seems likely to be the antidote to greed, that's ultimately not the case—even disposition is harmful. Anchoring fools us, as we've learned in this chapter, by establishing a context for our estimation of value that isn't valid. And we get pulled into the phantasy of novel products made by interesting companies with iconic founders, thinking that some of what makes them special will rub off on us. Unfortunately, that's not true either. In the next chapter we'll examine one of the most basic human desires: to be part of the group even if the group is wrong. We'll also look at how we overreact to bad news to the point that a portfolio of stocks that have done horribly in the recent past performs better than ones that seem unable to do wrong.

CHAPTER 3

COMPLEXITY

It was six times larger than the second-largest corporate bankruptcy in history, July 2002's enormous, fraud-fueled collapse of the telecommunications giant WorldCom. It was nearly ten times larger than number three, Enron's 2001 bankruptcy. When the investment bank Lehman Brothers filed for bankruptcy at one forty-five in the morning on Monday, September 15, 2008, its list of debts named more than a hundred thousand individuals and businesses and the total owed topped $613 billion. The petition listed Citibank as Lehman's biggest creditor and said the amount owed was "Approximately $138 billion." The bankruptcy was so enormous that the entire process would take more than a decade to unfold with professional fees paid to lawyers and caretakers surpassing $2 billion.

The stock market fell nearly 5 percent that day, closing more than 31 percent below the high it had reached less than a year before. Over the next six months, investors would discover just how much further it had to fall: another 43 percent before it finally bottomed out. The whole sickening ride would cut the value of the US stock market by more than half in less than eighteen months, a more devastating pullback than even the one at the start of the Great Depression.

The economy had been in distress for some time, even if it took more than a year for that to manifest in the stock market. All the signs had been there including a malignant, unstable boom in housing prices fueled by mortgage-backed securities and a new breed of mortgage, euphemistically called "subprime." Investors would later ask themselves if that was a clue about what was to come.

Little had changed in the mortgage market for decades since the introduction of the thirty-year mortgage in the 1930s. Few lenders offered subprime mortgages prior to 2000 and they were almost exclusively the province of borrowers with poor credit histories. Subprime loans were once shameful and rare, but in the first decade of the twenty-first century, they became more common as America's fixation with the virtues of home ownership and the ability to combine subprime mortgages in a sellable portfolio rinsed them clean of much of their former stigma.

When the Federal Reserve lowered interest rates to nearly zero in response to the collapse of the internet bubble and the September 11 attacks, global investors predictably went in search of higher yields than those offered by traditional Treasury notes and bonds. Investors discovered mortgage-backed securities and snapped them up and, as a result, trillions of dollars were injected into the mortgage market, making it possible for millions of Americans to become home owners. The result was astounding growth in home ownership rates, from below 50 percent in 1920 to just more than 60 percent in 1960, to the crest of the wave, 69 percent in 2005. Housing prices in the United States predictably rose as well, climbing 84 percent from the start of 2000 to their peak in July 2006—a compound gain of nearly 10 percent a year.

Housing prices peaked in 2006 but it was easy for investors to dismiss the subsequent decline as minor—prices fell just 1.1 percent between that peak and February 2007. Despite such a tiny decline, the problems began almost immediately. HSBC, one of the largest banks in the world, issued a warning about mortgage-backed securities in February 2007. Two months later, New Century Financial, one of the largest issuers of subprime mortgages, failed and filed for bankruptcy, throwing its 7,200 employees out of jobs. Presumably many of them had mortgages they could no longer pay. Then in July 2007 the investment bank Bear Stearns admitted to the investors in two of its mortgage-focused hedge funds that one of the funds had suffered a total loss of the $600 million invested while the other had blown through 91 percent of the nearly $1 billion invested in it. Despite all this, on July 19, 2007, just two days after Bear Stearns's admission, the Dow Jones Industrial Average would close above 14,000 for the very first time.

The home mortgage tends to be a wonderful investment for the lender. The property is pledged to ensure that the loan is repaid and as long as a sufficient down payment is made, there is very little potential for loss. The loan is a lot like buying a bond; the lender makes the initial outlay but then gets its principal returned every month along with interest. Some institutional investors recognized this and when they realized that the investment return more than accounted for any risk over and above that of government Treasury notes, they wondered if they couldn't buy an interest in a bundle of mortgages.

One problem loomed. While big institutional investors such as pension funds and life insurance companies would have liked to buy a portfolio of mortgages, before the 1980s they were prevented from doing so by their investment mandate which required that they invest only in instruments with the highest possible credit rating—which left just government notes, and their lower rate of return.

One solution to this conundrum would be for a bank to acquire a portfolio of mortgages and then divide the portfolio into slices. One slice would be the first to receive principal and interest payments and it would be the least risky. A second slice would be the next to receive principal and interest payments. The riskiest slice would be the last to receive principal and interest payments. Consistent with their risk, the first, safest, slice would pay to its owners the lowest interest rate but it would still be a rate that more than made up for any additional risk. The second slice would pay a slightly higher rate of interest. The last slice, the riskiest slice, would pay the highest rate of interest. These slices would be known as *tranches*, from the French word for "slice."

The first bundle of mortgages was divided like this in 1983. When the safest tranches were reviewed by the commercial rating agencies, such as Standard & Poor's and Moody's Investors Service, they received the absolute safest rating possible, the same rating enjoyed by US Treasury notes. This solved the problem for institutional investors. They could now buy these safest tranches and enjoy their superior return.

The mortgage market grew, but not just because owners of mortgage-backed securities were earning extra money. It grew because *everyone* was making more money. The original lenders were making money and the investment banks that bought their mortgages, bundled them, sliced them into tranches, and sold the tranches were making enormous amounts of money. That spurred them to buy more mortgages which meant different types of mortgages. When all the prime borrowers had been tapped, the banks pushed lenders to grant mortgages to less creditworthy borrowers. The result was that creditworthiness for those who were able to get a home mortgage slid from "rock solid," to "subprime," to "barely hanging on." These latter mortgages were made to borrowers who often didn't even provide evidence of employment and income, yet they were euphemistically called subprime mortgages, as if they were just a tiny bit shy of the standards necessary for prime status. Often they were junk.

How can an investor make intelligent decisions when they're investing in companies with stunningly complex products, like in biotechnology, or in financial vehicles that are just as byzantine and difficult to understand? The first step is to avoid behavioral biases such as getting pulled into an investment solely because the company, product, or founder is phantastic. Another step is to avoid the overconfidence we visited in the first chapter. It is ironic that overconfidence tends to be strongest when investing in something that is difficult to understand.

We'll visit some new biases that were particularly evident

in 2008. Herding was probably the most harmful as investors who didn't fully appreciate what was going on followed others who had no additional insight merely because following along seemed like the thing to do. Another prevalent bias was overreacting to negative and unexpected news. When an august US investment bank files for the largest bankruptcy in history, one that is six-times larger than the next biggest ever, it seems that it would be impossible to overreact, but investors did exactly that, and many paid the price.

No investment bank that survived what was to come would be hurt more than Merrill Lynch and they were the ones that started the unraveling of the whole mess. The nearly hundred-year-old firm had lent $400 million to two Bear Stearns hedge funds. In this situation, the term "hedge fund" is a misnomer because nothing about the funds was hedged in any modern sense of that word. The first was called the High-Grade Structured Credit Strategies Fund and, like its sister fund, which added "Enhanced Leverage" to its name, the general strategy was to take a small investment and then borrow a bunch of additional money. With that money in hand, the fund would buy mortgage-backed securities because they paid more in interest than it cost to borrow the money.

What Bear Stearns overlooked was risk. What happens when the price of the mortgage-backed securities falls because the mortgages they contain go into foreclosure? This is what was happening in the American housing market in early 2007 and the first warning had been sounded months earlier by

HSBC. So, on June 15, 2007, Merrill seized $400 million in mortgage-backed securities owned by the Bear Stearns's hedge funds. They served as collateral for the loans Merrill had made and rather than wait for Bear Stearns to decide if it was going to unwind some of the fund's holdings and reduce the risk, Merrill chose to act. Unfortunately, this was the only time Merrill was decisive; the firm would end up losing more than $50 billion in the mortgage crisis. Just as the investors who insisted to Professor Shiller immediately after the 1987 crash that they had seen it coming, even if their trading records prove they did not, it would be easy for us to look back at Merrill Lynch's actions, and lack of action, with the benefit of hindsight and wonder what its leadership was thinking. Or not thinking. But instead of indulging in that exercise, the lesson investors might learn is that, in the moment, as it's all going on, it's impossible to know what is going to happen next. The best an investor can do is the right thing or the most logical thing at the moment, and that means understanding the behavioral biases that want us to do the wrong thing.

After an interim high of just more than 14,000 in the Dow Jones Industrial Average in July 2007, the parade of bad economic news continued. Countrywide Financial was a giant lender that had offered mortgages to only the most creditworthy buyers for three decades before sacrificing its standards in pursuit of market share. It happened slowly, almost imperceptivity at first, but steadily until the company saw profits slip and warned shareholders that there was more trouble ahead. Then on August 1, the two Bear Stearns hedge funds officially filed for bankruptcy. Bear Stearns's copresident was forced to resign due to the fiasco and its new president felt the need to send a note to clients reassuring them that the firm was still solvent.

On August 3, the public learned that the number of Americans who held a job had declined for the first time in nearly four years. On August 9, French bank BNP Paribas halted redemptions from its own mortgage-focused hedge funds due to a "complete evaporation of liquidity" in the market for subprime mortgages. The litany of disappointing news continued one week later when the Dow closed more than 1,150 points below the all-time high it had reached just twenty trading days earlier. Later in August, Lehman Brothers, an investment bank that could trace its beginnings to 1844 but which would cease to exist in just thirteen months, announced it would shutter its retail mortgage subsidiary, while, separately, Countrywide Financial accepted a $2 billion funding lifeline from commercial banking behemoth Bank of America. Then on the last day of August, Federal Reserve Chairman Ben Bernanke, a Harvard- and MIT-educated academic who had come to prominence by studying the causes of, and responses to, the Great Depression—warned in unambiguous language that the problems for investors in subprime mortgages were going to get worse.

The pace of bad economic news only accelerated after Wall Street returned to work following the Labor Day weekend of 2007. On September 5, Apple shares fell more than 5 percent when the company announced it would cut the price of its most expensive iPhone by one-third. On September 20, Bear Stearns acknowledged that its hedge fund misadventure had crushed the bank's overall results for the quarter and that profits had dropped by more than two-thirds. On the first day of October, the Swiss bank UBS announced it would write down the value of subprime mortgages it owned by as much as $3.4 billion—a stunning admission for a financial institution that prided itself on controlling risk. Four days later, Merrill Lynch, the quintessential American investment bank and stockbroker, announced that the value of subprime mortgages in its own portfolio had declined by $5.5 billion. Whoever had seen the problem coming had been right.

In spite of this stream of bad news, the stock market had recovered its losses from the first half of August and bulled its way higher, proving the adage that the stock market is not the economy. Both the S&P 500 Index and the Dow Jones Industrial Average made new all-time highs on October 9, 2007. It was an impressive performance.

These latest high-water marks were actually a result of things being so bad; earlier that day the Federal Reserve had released the minutes of a recent meeting at which it had decided to cut interest rates more than expected because "the committee unanimously believed that such a large cut in borrowing costs was necessary to stop problems in the credit markets [which included mortgage-backed securities]." Perversely, investors bought stocks on the news that rates were likely to be even lower in the near future because things were so bad in the mortgage market.

Investors were beginning to realize that while it was easy to know the value of a stock portfolio—even in 1720, Isaac Newton could learn where South Sea Company stock was trading twice a day—it was often simply impossible to know the value of a portfolio of the sort of mortgage-backed securities that had tripped up HSBC, Bear Stearns, UBS, and Merrill Lynch, just as it is impossible for a home owner to know the precise value of their home. The day after the market made its new all-time high, the investment bank Goldman Sachs announced that 7 percent of its assets, more than $72 billion worth, were labeled as 'level 3' meaning they was so esoteric and traded so infrequently that it was difficult for even for the brightest minds at Goldman Sachs to value them accurately. Much of that $72 billion was mortgage-backed securities and it was more than one and a half times the total shareholder's equity the investment giant would have on its balance sheet at the end of the year.

If it was difficult to value these arcane assets accurately then even bankers at the same firm could have wildly divergent estimates of the value of mortgage-backed securities. The *Wall Street Journal* reported in October 2007 that when a hedge fund manager at one firm realized the previous March that falling housing prices and climbing mortgage delinquencies meant the mortgage-backed securities in his fund had dropped in value, he wrote down, or marked down, their value, saying, "I'm marking to where I could reasonably sell them." Doing so is imminently prudent but other managers at his fund's parent owned the same mortgage-backed bonds and wanted the freedom to value them at much higher prices. Their motives were not likely of a pure heart and their colleague's much lower valuations would be embarrassing and inconvenient if they were to maintain their more optimistic, and personally lucrative, valuations. Their more prudent colleague was shown the door.

Isaac and the other speculators caught up in the South Sea bubble had been enchanted by their newfound ability to precisely and frequently price their shares. The natural next step was to guess where shares were headed next. That led to over-trading. Speculators in internet stocks had done the same, with many believing that Yahoo, AOL, Pets.com, Webvan, and even the defunct commercial printer Webworld were headed higher as the instantaneous price dissemination the internet itself offered turned the whole thing into a video game. Market transparency in 2007 had taken an enormous step backward. On the same day that Goldman Sachs announced it had ended the third quarter of 2007 with $72 billion in level 3 assets, those securities which traded so infrequently that they were nearly impossible to value, a Goldman analyst pointed out that "way less than half" of all securities in the United States traded on exchanges with competing parties setting objective prices in arm's-length transactions.

The dangers faced by the average investor in 2008 and 2009 were absolutely unique. At their heart, previous stock market crashes and bear markets had to do with the value of stocks. In 1720, the 1920s, the 1970s, 1987, and 2000, investors could debate their value. This time the core of the debate revolved around the value of opaque instruments such as mortgage-backed securities and their malevolently esoteric offspring, including credit default swaps and synthetic collateralized debt obligations. Average investors would be stung by the decline in stock prices and behavioral quirks would work to further undermine their investing returns. The astonishing and dangerous element in October 2007 was that average investors might believe many different times over the next eighteen months, that this was the bottom, that the news had been bad and the market had dropped, but that this would be the low point. But the bad news didn't stop; interest rates had been too low for too long, making mortgage-backed securities too enticing. What's more, housing prices had grown too fast while the investment vehicles themselves were too obscure and buried too deeply in the balance sheets of too many firms around the world. At the same time, the leaders of those firms couldn't fathom the full extent of their risk so bad news continued to gradually trickle out and the market would fall some more.

Citigroup was just one example, albeit an extreme one. The parent of one of the largest banks in the world would see its stock price crushed by the crisis; from its high of $562.80 in 2007 to its low of just $9.70 in 2009, it would lose more than 98 percent. The causes of Citibank's troubles were overconfidence and underappreciation of the risks involved in opaque products. Even after the Bear Stearns mortgage-focused hedge funds collapsed, Citigroup thought the likelihood of defaulting on any of its $100 billion of mortgage-backed securities was "less than .01 percent." One one-hundredth of 1 percent of $100 billion is a mere $10 million. But another executive was even more (over)confident, claiming that Citi "would never lose a penny" on the mortgages it held. Between writing down the value of mortgage-backed securities that Citigroup owned and payments made to settle investigations and lawsuits, Citi's total losses from its mortgage business would total approximately $50 billion.

Merrill Lynch similarly thought it was business as usual through 2007. Rather than reduce risk, it often larded on more. It had plowed money into a new Indonesian coal mine in August then entered into an agreement to buy all the coal produced by the mine for its first several years. By the end of September, Merrill had purchased a huge stake in a German insurance company.

All this happened despite clear warning signs. At the same time Merrill was adding risk in 2007, it was downgrading the prospects for Citigroup, Lehman Brothers, and Bear Stearns due to fears about the slowing market for mortgage-backed securities. In a turnabout, at the end of the month, Lehman Brothers would cut its earnings estimates for all of the other investment banks, including Merrill Lynch. Then, during the first week in October, Merrill announced that $5.5 billion write-down in the value of its holdings of mortgage-backed securities. Yet during the last week in October, Merrill announced that while shareholders were taking it on the chin, employees were being taken care of. Merrill's compensation ratio, the percentage of revenue that funds wages, bonuses, and benefits, would shoot up from 49 percent, the industry standard, to a gaudy 58 percent.

The job of the average investor is not to guess what the stock market is going to do next month. Why not? Because it's impossible to know. We'll learn just how impossible in chapter 4. Instead, the job of the average investor is to assume that the market will appreciate over time—we'll also learn just how safe a bet this is in chapter 4—and to invest in a manner appropriate for their age while working to prevent these behavioral quirks and biases, including overconfidence, from hurting their returns.

One thing investors *should* do in the moment is to go easy on themselves. If 2008 taught us anything, it's that many highly paid professionals with impressive pedigrees at elite investment banks got pretty much everything wrong. It may seem that you should have known what was about to happen but that's a trick your mind plays on you. If you had a sensible portfolio that was appropriately diversified, kept investing even when it looked ugly, and didn't give in to behavioral quirks and biases, then you did as well as you could do. If those things weren't true in 2008, or in one of the subsequent bear markets, then your job is to make certain they are true next time. You are the key, not the stocks you pick.

On October 10, 2007, the day after that new all-time high, the S&P 500 index slid a miniscule 2.68 points, or less than 0.2 percent. The loss had nothing to do with mortgages, subprime or not. Instead, the Boeing Company had announced that its new 787 Dreamliner wide-body commercial jet would be delayed by an additional six months due to assembly problems while the aluminum maker Alcoa released disappointing results for the previous quarter and the energy giant Chevron warned that refining margins were under pressure and their profits would suffer. The market was still up just more than 10 percent for the year, a solid if not spectacular performance. Despite the minor hiccups that these blue-chip companies had encountered, the underlying problem was mortgages and the banks that owned them, but the signal was being lost in the noise. This is another reason investors should go easy on themselves and focus on their biases.

We know at this point that nobody understood the magnitude of the global problem created by the combination of mortgage-backed securities, leverage used by financial firms such as Bear Stearns, and the potential impact on mainstream stock markets. At the same time, we know that individual investors could not have been expected to understand the magnitude of the problem. All of this is obvious from the makeup of the group formed in October 2007, just after the peak in the US stock market, to take over Northern Rock, a troubled mortgage lender based in England, just south of the border with Scotland. The consortium was led by the iconoclastic British entrepreneur Richard Branson but it included insurance giant American International Group (AIG). The idea that AIG would consider paying money to get more exposure to the mortgage business in October 2007 is stunning given that in early July, when one AIG senior official was asked about the mortgage exposure the company already had, his response was, "We're fucked, basically."

In 1997, AIG agreed to insure something entirely new against loss: a bundle of bank loans. That led to the insurer covering bundles and tranches of mortgages against loss, overly confident that it understood the risks and what it was insuring. AIG was wrong in the same way the overconfident bankers at Citigroup were wrong. Both Citigroup and AIG had thought it was impossible to lose money because home values had never dropped across the entire country at the same time. Home prices had occasionally shown systemic weakness in certain regions but never nationally, so AIG wrote more of this insurance than anyone else: more than $500 billion on a variety of assets and $78 billion on mortgages. And the geniuses at AIG bet wrong. The risk they took was rooted in the idea that something that was only remotely possible—home prices and mortgage values falling in sync—was impossible. And they bet the company on it. Now the insured expected to be reimbursed for their losses.

On July 27, 2007, Goldman Sachs demanded payment of $1.8 billion from AIG for the idiotic insurance it had written on a bundle of home mortgages. This was the first time anyone had demanded AIG make good on the tens of billions of dollars' worth of mortgage insurance it had written—insurance that AIG thought could never cost it even a single dollar in an orgy of overconfidence. Goldman Sachs's claim was so unexpected and so large that one AIG executive described it by saying it "hit out of the blue, and a fucking number that's well bigger than we ever planned for." On September 11, 2007, Goldman Sachs came calling for another $1.5 billion from AIG. The idea that in October AIG could agree to play a major role in Branson's plans to save Northern Rock despite its own private troubles with mortgages—and the public crises engulfing HSBC, Bear Stearns, Merrill Lynch, and Northern Rock itself—is unfathomable unless we remember that investors are great at paying attention to what's going on when markets are good and horrible when markets are bad. Things were bad for AIG, yet it didn't seem to be paying much attention.

Investors' attention is a finite resource and it becomes scarcer still when markets are falling. When the market is struggling, many investors cope with their anguish by simply not logging into their investment accounts after market declines, as if not seeing the damage will make it go away. It's a childish habit that researchers call the ostrich effect, after the gawky birds who are known to stick their heads in the sand when danger approaches. If I can't see the danger, the ostrich seems to believe, then it doesn't exist.

Much of the ostrich effect is tied to the idea that it's simply more pleasurable—researchers use the word *hedonic*—to expend the finite resource of attention and check an account balance when the balance is increasing, and is less pleasurable when it is falling. The pleasure when stocks are higher is not nearly as great if an investor simply looks at her account balance as it would be if she gave into the disposition effect and sold a winner, but it's pleasurable nonetheless. This is where many behavioral biases come together to hurt an investor's performance. They pay less attention to their portfolio when there are things to be done such as putting idle cash to work or harvesting tax losses or rebalancing to make certain the portfolio is appropriately diversified. Sometimes they make one of the worst mistakes imaginable and sell it all at the bottom or stop investing entirely. There were certainly things for the professionals at Bear Stearns, Lehman Brothers, AIG, and Merrill Lynch to be doing to mitigate the damage in their portfolios of mortgage-backed securities. But the extra pain from each additional dollar lost as explained by prospect theory, is felt and status quo bias kicks in. Even the hard-nosed and sharp-elbowed traders on Wall Street refused to act.

In one study of a hundred thousand retirement accounts, investors were more than twice as likely to log in to their account if the broad stock market had gained ground on the previous day than they were if it had dropped; and they were three times more likely to execute a trade if the market had been up the previous day in what is likely an echo from the disposition effect. This change in attention takes place over daily, weekly, and monthly time frames and the ostrich effect is a stable personal characteristic—meaning investors tend to exhibit it or not, but they don't switch back and forth. Executives at AIG seemed to have fully embraced the ostrich effect if they were interested in getting more exposure to mortgages by being part of the group that would bail out Northern Rock.

What sort of investor is most likely to exhibit the ostrich effect? Men and wealthier investors are especially prone to it. Wealthier investors may be more susceptible because the absolute numbers are larger. The tendency of men to pay more attention when markets are strong, meaning portfolios are doing well, and to pay less attention when markets are weak, almost certainly fuels their overconfidence, which leads to overtrading and inferior results. And these "ostriches" tend to underestimate risk, because the only time they really look at the stock market is when it's trending higher.

The most damaging aspect of investors having limited attention is the way they pick individual stocks. We've already discussed how investors tend to focus on stocks that are headquartered near their home or operate in the industry in which they are employed. But investors also tend to be net buyers of stocks with abnormally high trading volume or with an abnormally large percentage change, positive or negative, on the previous day. One group of individual investors at a large discount brokerage was twenty-times more likely to buy the large-cap stocks with the highest volume on the previous day than to sell them. Those investors were three times more likely to buy the stocks which displayed the best returns on the previous day than to sell them. Investors also buy stocks simply for the companies' having been in the news the day before. (Recall the story of Webworld.) In case it bears repeating, the authors of the study note wryly, "The attention-driven buying patterns we document here do not generate superior returns."

When a stock appears in the news or grabs investors' attention in other ways, they will often do a little rudimentary research and Google is the place many start. That means Google search volume can be a good proxy for the amount of attention a stock is getting among individual investors. One study using data from 2004 to 2008 in Brazil, showed that an increase in Google search volume for a stock was followed by a slightly negative return for the stock in the following week. The measured impact is small but important to understand. Any market-moving news will be acted on immediately by professional traders, so bullish news will have already generated the expected rally by the time individual investors hear it, turn to Google, do what passes for research, decide to trade, log into their accounts, and execute their trades. Our individual investor buys near the top of the market then watches their newly owned shares fall in price as the first to buy, or longer-term shareholders susceptible to the disposition effect, take their profits.

It isn't just eye-popping one-day performance or exceptional volume that draws investors' attention and their investment dollars. Higher advertising spending by a company, everything else staying the same, leads to both individuals and institutional investors being more likely to own the stock.

Advertising is effective for many businesses but as all those ads for internet companies from the 2000 Super Bowl demonstrate, sometimes advertising is just a conspicuous waste of money. Gross advertising spending certainly isn't a reliable measure of a company's prospects.

How else can we know that investors have a limited pool of attention to draw from? Every publicly traded company reports its financial results four times a year. These announcements tend to cluster in the weeks just after the end of the calendar quarter, so during the middle of April or July there are often days which have dozens of important earnings announcements. Some other companies, which are on a different fiscal calendar and have different reporting cycles, may report in the middle of August or November, and may be the only important company announcing results that day. We know that investors have a limited amount of attention because when a company is just one of many reporting on any particular day, and it reports earnings that are surprisingly divergent from what the stock market had been expecting, it will experience a smaller reaction than that seen for companies with similar earnings surprises reported on days when there are few earnings announcements. The same sort of thing happens depending on the day of the week the announcement occurs on. For example, earnings announcements that take place on Friday, when investors are likely thinking about other things, result in a smaller reaction in the stock price.

None of these attention-grabbing traits is likely to be helpful in a world filled with investment analysts and computer algorithms working across the entire roster of all investable securities to find the next hidden investment gem. By the time everyone hears about a stock because of extreme volume or a huge move in price or a TV ad, the odds of it having undiscovered value are infinitesimally small.

The S&P ended 2007 with just a 3.5 percent return having given back much of the gain it had enjoyed as recently as October. But the market was lucky to hang on to even that small gain. During the week before Christmas, the investment bank Morgan Stanley told the world that it had lost $3.6 billion dollars in the previous quarter, due entirely to a write-down of $9.4 billion in the value of mortgage assets it owned. It was the first time Morgan Stanley had posted a quarterly loss in years, going back to before the bursting of the internet bubble. The only good news as the year hobbled to a close came from Merrill Lynch which announced on Christmas day that it had raised more than $6 billion in new capital from foreign investors.

In a harbinger of what was to come, the S&P lost 1.4 percent on the first trading day of 2008. Not once would the index close in positive territory for the year. However, even before the market closed that day there was bad news. Merrill Lynch announced that it had been forced to give a $50 million discount on two life insurance companies it was selling to a Dutch company. It was selling the companies to free up $800 million in capital at a time when other parts of Merrill were committing to buy the entire output of the Indonesian coal mine it had acquired the previous year. On the same day, it was reported that Merrill, despite having raised all that money the preceding week, was in talks with sovereign wealth funds in the Middle

East and China for another giant infusion of cash. There would be new reports that Merrill was trying to raise $925 million from a bank in Japan before the week was out.

It wouldn't be nearly enough because on January 17 Merrill announced its results for the fourth quarter of 2007. It was a net loss of $9.8 billion thanks to $16.7 billion in write-downs on the value of mortgages it held. Merrill's new CEO, John Thain, called the results "unacceptable" in the epitome of understatement. Soon Merrill would announce it had raised another $5 billion from funds in Korea and Kuwait. The company had raised a total of $12.8 billion but that didn't yet make up for the losses of $16.7 billion it had admitted to on its subprime mortgages— mortgages it couldn't unload at any price. Total subprime-related losses for all global banks now exceeded $100 billion, and it was still the first month of 2008.

It became a race for all the investment banks. They had to raise additional capital and they had to face up to the losses they were incurring on the subprime mortgages they owned. It had been easy for the banks to bundle mortgages and sell them when other interest rates were low because the bundles offered a few extra percentage points of yield; everyone had wanted them. Now the banks were stuck with what had been in their pipelines and previous buyers wanted to sell what they already owned. Nobody was willing to take any of it at any price. It had been nearly a year since HSBC alerted the world to the declining value of subprime mortgages and five months since the French bank BNP Paribas acknowledged a "complete evaporation of liquidity" in the market for subprime mortgages.

As the banks raced to raise enough money to stay solvent,

they also faced a bevy of lawsuits from the supposedly sophisticated institutional investors who had bought the mortgage-backed securities the banks had peddled. With the additional interest and the promises that they were the safest securities available, they had been an easy sale, even to those for whom they were completely inappropriate. During the middle of January, the city of Springfield, Massachusetts, a home to 150,000 on the banks of the Connecticut River and best known as the birthplace of basketball, warned Merrill Lynch that it was ready to sue over the near-total loss it had sustained on $14 million of mortgage-backed securities it purchased in spring 2007. Springfield had been part of the herd, buying mortgage-backed securities it didn't understand. City administrators admitted they couldn't have understood what they were buying because they didn't read the prospectus explaining what they were buying before making the purchase. We know they didn't read the prospectus before making the purchase because they didn't even *receive* the prospectus until months later.

The average investor likes to be part of the herd. Some researchers say it's because we're wired to follow the crowd when faced with uncertainty. Others say that simply being part of a crowd changes the way in which we perceive the world and that change reinforces the herding instinct. Herding happens in markets when investors choose to imitate what they see other investors doing rather than go their own way. They often do so because they believe those other investors are smarter or better informed.

Sometimes being part of the herd even induces people to break the rules.

About fourteen tons of petrified wood is stolen by visitors to Arizona's Petrified Forest National Park every year. With nearly a million visitors a year, the losses add up even though each individual theft is small. In an effort to stop these thefts, Park Service officials erected signs but psychologists wondered if the signs weren't part of the problem. The signs complained about the volume of thefts but then seemed to dismiss their seriousness by pointing out that they occurred "mostly a small piece at a time." Maybe the signs were normalizing theft, suggesting that visitors should feel free to "join the herd" and help themselves if they took just a small piece. Sure enough, thefts on one trail declined by one-third when researchers removed the signs from that trail entirely. When the signs normalizing theft were replaced by ones that did not mention the amount of theft and included an image of a single hand stealing a piece of petrified wood behind the generic red-circle-and-backslash "no" symbol, the amount of theft dropped by 80 percent. Thefts declined when it was no longer okay to be part of the herd.

The same thing often occurs with investors, many of whom would inexplicably prefer to be part of the herd than be right. This sometimes leads to bubbles as investors follow along and the herding becomes extreme. Doing so works for a while and then it doesn't, often in spectacular fashion.

The need to be accepted as part of the group, even if the group is wrong, is part of the social dynamic of trading, particularly when times are tough. One study focusing on Korean investors during the 1997–98 Asian economic crisis demonstrated that a wide assortment of investors who had acted independently of one another before the crisis suddenly began mimicking one another once it hit. The result was herding and positive-feedback trading which pushed the worst performing stocks too low and the best-performing stocks too high. For a trader who had gone their own way—what some might call a contrarian—the difference in performance was significant. Contrarians outperformed the herd over every monthly time frame from one month to six months during the crisis. Their excess one-month return was more than 9 percentage points. Going your own way can be tough to do because it is deeply uncomfortable. But those who do will be rewarded.

How do we know that most people would rather be part of the herd and underperform than go it alone and outperform? In another study, groups of five people were all shown the same pair of three-dimensional shapes from different perspectives. Each subject was supposed to determine if the two shapes were identical or different. Then everyone in the group would see how the others had answered. Those answers were displayed on a screen next to the participant's name and photo. To make the exercise even more personal, group members were introduced to one another at the start of the session and they played friendly practice rounds together before the actual testing started.

During testing, each participant's brain was supposedly being scanned by MRI. But in a twist, only one person in each group was an actual subject; the other members were actors who had been instructed to purposefully give the wrong answer half the time. When the real test subject's answer was in conflict with the group consensus, even if it was correct, their MRI showed heightened activity in the right amygdala, a part of the brain responsible for negative emotions. The real test subject would change their correct answer to the wrong answer about 27 percent of the time if it was preferred by the rest of the group. In this situation, standing apart from the crowd didn't induce the intellectual question "Why are they getting it wrong?" but an emotional response: "What's wrong with me?" The need to be part of the group, the herd, is a powerful one and it's driven by emotion, not intellect. This explains why Isaac Newton fell for it. This explains why so many investors in internet stocks in 2000 fell for the need to be part of the herd. It explains why so many bought houses they couldn't afford just a few years later. And as they all demonstrated, it is bad for our stock market returns.

Herding is particularly dangerous on the downside of a bear market or stock market crash when the ability to think independently is simultaneously elusive and crucial. If investors come to believe, as one, that the damage will continue, in the way a flock of starlings in flight seem to move as one, then the bear market or crash will continue. When the cost of processing information increases, as it seems to do when stocks are falling in price and our ability to focus wanes, then the temptation to herd only increases.

In a flock of starlings, the synchronized swooping and climbing is called murmuration and it can be mesmerizing to watch. It is thought to offer protection from predators such as falcons which might have trouble identifying a single bird among the rolling waves of hundreds or thousands. Each individual starling pays attention to the movement of just seven other birds and demonstrates, as one researcher described it, a "remarkable ability to maintain cohesion as a group in highly uncertain environments and with limited, noisy information." Unfortunately, investor herding offers no such protection.

The housing bubble itself had been caused by a sort of herding as potential home buyers watched actual home buyers and decided to join the crowd, thinking that those who had come before had done the grueling work of planning and budgeting so it must be all right. Members of the herd bought houses they couldn't afford and now they were defaulting.

Many traders will talk about using momentum strategies to jump into the stock market once a trend is under way. Momentum strategies are simply the embodiment of herd mentality dressed up in vaguely academic language in an attempt to lend legitimacy to the whole approach.

There is one circumstance when herding is logical, at least for professional money managers. If you're paying someone else to invest money on your behalf they can have an aberrant incentive to follow the herd, even if they believe the herd is wrong like the test subjects comparing shapes while in the MRI. How so? If your fund manager goes his own way and loses money while the herd is making money, he'll get all the blame and you'll likely take your business elsewhere. If he instead makes money when others are losing money then self-attribution bias will take hold and you'll tend to pat yourself on the back for picking the right manager while the manager gets just a portion of the credit. But if the fund manager is part of the herd, losing money when others are losing money and making it when others are making it, there's less reputational risk. In this vein, some money managers describe a bubble as "something I get fired for not owning."

Being part of the herd wasn't lucrative for investors in January 2008. The S&P lost more than 6 percent that month and after falling nearly 2 percent on January 8 it was more than 10 percent below its all-time high, officially reaching "correction" territory. Some investors seemed to understand the scope of the problem but that did not include the management of Lehman Brothers. The company would cease to exist just seven and a half months later. But on January 29, as that horrible month was ending, Lehman decided to raise its dividend and buy back up to $6.25 billion worth of its own shares.

February 2008 wasn't much better for the stock market and it was even worse for AIG. The S&P lost another 3.5 percent meaning it was already down more than 9 percent for the year. At the end of the month, AIG finally admitted what everyone knew; it had insured bundles of mortgages the banks had assembled against any loss, overly confident that it knew what it was doing. AIG was finally facing up to its problems but Joseph Cassano, the executive in charge of the division that had written all this insurance, thought the company's liability was $1.2 billion. AIG's outside auditor contended that the problem was much bigger and was pushing for a write-down of $5 billion. After sharpening its pencil and actually calculating the impairment, AIG announced a write-down of more than $11 billion on February 28. Its stock price lost more than 10 percent during the last two days of February but it ended the month only 35 percent below its highest level from the previous year.

The S&P lost just a little ground in March 2008 but investors were whipsawed by the stream of news. On the last day of February, Federal Reserve chairman Bernanke had warned that he wouldn't be surprised if some banks failed due to the crisis. Banks seized the assets of another mortgage-focused hedge fund early in the month, just as they had grabbed the assets of those Bear Stearns hedge funds the previous year. A few days later, Citigroup put out a statement that it was comfortable with its capital levels. The next day the stock fell 4.4 percent. Later that week, Bear Stearns confirmed that the deal for a much-needed infusion of cash from a Chinese bank was still on, even though they had been forced to adjust its terms. On the same day, Citigroup announced it would close some bank branches in its weaker regions—a move that was welcomed even if it was borne of a desperate need to cut expenses. On March 8 it was reported that the Federal Bureau of Investigation was investigating subprime lender Countrywide Financial for possible securities fraud. Lehman Brothers leaked the news that it would cut its staff by 5 percent in a reversal from its recent profligate dividend increase and announcement of stock buybacks.

Then on Tuesday, March 11, stocks rallied by nearly 4 percent on news that the Federal Reserve would inject additional liquidity into the financial sector. The good news seemed to continue the following morning when Alan Schwartz, Bear Stearns's CEO, went on TV and reassured investors that his company was sound and that he was "comfortable" it had generated a profit during the current quarter.

The very next day, Bear Stearns's lawyers were in front of the US Treasury, confessing that the company was, notwithstanding Schwartz's reassurance, in dire financial straits. It is simply impossible to reconcile Schwartz's public assurance with the company's actual condition and its conversation with the US Treasury. American investment banks don't die a lingering death; they go from more or less healthy, with ample credit available, to dead. Investment banks in 2008 funded their ongoing operations with short-term, overnight borrowing that had to be refreshed each day. When other institutions refused to roll over the lending, the bank failed, literally overnight. The path of a troubled bank like Bear Stearns would resemble that of the character in Ernest Hemingway's novel *The Sun Also Rises*, who, when asked how he'd gone broke, answered, "Two ways, gradually and then suddenly."

By the end of the week, Bear Stearns had admitted failure and been acquired at a fire-sale price by JPMorgan Chase & Co., one of the country's oldest and largest financial institutions, but with the assistance of the Federal Reserve—an indication that as the lender of last resort, the Fed was willing to step in when needed. The stock market fell by just 1.6 percent that day, a muted response to the failure of one of only five American investment banks, albeit the smallest of the five. But the response was probably more a reaction to the extraordinary steps taken by the Federal Reserve than a recognition of the scope of the problems.

Then, on March 18, Lehman Brothers reported fourth-quarter net income of $489 million, 12.5 percent more than expected. In a cautionary tale about the opacity of prices in the mortgage-backed securities market, the freedom that holders of those securities had in valuing them, and the folly of an individual investor trying to glean market intelligence from a corporate earnings announcement, the company would file for bankruptcy in just 181 days.

The month brought more news from Lehman Brothers when it admitted it might have lost $250 million—more than half what it had earned in the previous quarter and money it could barely afford to lose—due to a fraud in Japan involving forged documents and financing for hospitals that were buying medical equipment that didn't exist.

March ended on a Monday, with the S&P having lost just 0.6 percent, an expression of the back-and-forth nature of the month's news. The fact that the loss was that small suggested that traders were already experiencing information overload.

Just as attention is a finite resource, so too is the ability to wade through financial data and make informed choices. With the avalanche of terrifying news stories and grim financial figures in early 2008, it was clear most investors were overwhelmed. Information overload is related to issues such as the ostrich effect and availability bias, but it is also easier to mitigate. A financially literate investor *can* avoid information overload during a crash or bear market by learning good investment habits when markets are calm.

Investors predictably rely on rules of thumb and short-cuts, what researchers call heuristics, to make decisions when suffering from information overload. Heuristics are a useful time-saving tool but they're also vulnerable to the many behavioral biases we've discussed. During information overload, investors become particularly susceptible to whoever is shouting the loudest or to stocks grabbing the most attention because they're trading a tremendous amount of volume or fluctuating wildly. Investors are more likely to join the herd rather than go their own way when they're experiencing information overload and they're less likely to be satisfied with their decisions even if they're the correct ones. For this reason, too much information can be as bad for decision-making as too little.

One study of information overload gave test subjects two choices: they could either make asset-allocation decisions for a hypothetical retirement account from a list of mutual funds or they could just stick the entire sum in a money market fund. The money market fund would be safe and would eliminate the burden of decision-making but it would generate very little return and therefore would be a horrible selection for a retirement account. The mutual funds offered included a range of asset classes and strategies and the researchers provided strategy and performance details for each one. The specifics of each fund had been borrowed from real-life funds so they represented actual products but the names had been changed to avoid any bias or familiarity. Each test subject also completed a ten-question test to gauge their financial literacy.

In one test, the subjects were offered as few as six choices of mutual funds. In another, they could choose from as many as sixty. Even when just six alternatives were offered, those with the lowest amount of financial literacy reached a point of information overload as demonstrated by throwing up their hands and selecting the default option of the money market fund ten times more often (20 percent versus 2 percent) than the most financially knowledgeable participants. Maybe most distressing, while reducing the number of investment options significantly reduced feelings of information overload among the most financially literate in the test, presenting only six choices had virtually no impact among the least financially literate. They were overloaded either way.

Information overload has a detrimental impact on investment results because it leads to investors taking the path of least resistance. They tend to pick the easiest option, like the money market fund in this study. Information overload also accentuates the status quo bias and inertia, and neither is rarely optimal. But it's easy to understand investors becoming overwhelmed when a crashing market and failing banks lead the news every day. The key to avoiding information overload is financial literacy.

Too often, when we think of financial literacy we imagine dissecting complicated financial reports. The truth is that most investors can improve their financial literacy by focusing on a few basic concepts. The Financial Industry Regulatory Authority (FINRA) is responsible for regulating exchanges and brokerage firms and it offers a simple, six-question test to gauge financial literacy. The questions cover topics such as compound interest, the impact of inflation on savings, the relationship between changes in interest rates and bond prices, different mortgages, and the impact of diversifying investments on the amount of risk assumed. None of the questions is very challenging but for the general population who takes the test the average number of correct answers is just three. So, the best way to improve financial literacy, at least for novices, is to focus on these basic concepts. Additional information on each of these topics is readily available in the traditional media or online. Those seeking to increase their financial literacy would be best served by thinking less about the hottest stock right now or how some charismatic CEO makes them feel, and more about these simple concepts.

The Dow lost more than 10 percent in June 2008, its worst month since September 2002 when it was still recovering from the bursting of the internet bubble and the 9/11 attacks. Standard & Poor's had started the month by cutting its credit ratings on the big banks. Then the unemployment rate jumped to 5.5 percent, its highest level in four years. On the ninth, Lehman Brothers was forced to preannounce its results for the current quarter as the company finally came to grips with reality. The loss totaled $2.8 billion and Lehman Brothers stock got slammed, losing 8.7 percent that day as more than 168 million shares were traded making Lehman one of the most active issues on the New York Stock Exchange. If either the huge percentage move or the enormous volume brought Lehman to investors' attention and they bought it, they would come to regret it. Lehman stock closed the day at $29.48. It would never trade that high again. Lehman Brothers, which had started as a general store in Montgomery, Alabama, would see its nearly 165 years of history undone in just 98 days.

Merrill Lynch was another American investment bank with a proud tradition although Merrill was probably best known for its "thundering herd" of retail stockbrokers. Not only had the company survived the Great Depression, it had also changed the landscape for stockbrokers after World War II by paying them a salary high enough to eliminate the need to churn accounts to generate commissions. Merrill courted average investors, not just the rich, and introduced those investors to Wall Street in the 1950s and 1960s at the same moment they were starting to accumulate wealth. Merrill was one of the first investment banks to go public itself and in the 1980s and 1990s it expanded its investment banking activities. In the next decade it would continue to push, this time becoming one of the biggest firms in the business of buying mortgages, bundling them into securities, and selling those securities to investors hungry for yield.

Now, in 2008, Merrill Lynch was continuing to raise money and sell off assets in a furious effort to remain solvent because the mortgages that remained on its books couldn't be sold even as they continued to drop in value.

The whole subprime mess shifted subtly from financial to criminal in the middle of June. On June 19, the FBI arrested 406 mortgage bankers and real estate developers as part of a crackdown on mortgage fraud that totaled more than $1 billion. The same day, the two managers of the now-defunct Bear Stearns hedge funds were arrested and charged with trying to retain existing investors, and lure new ones, by misstating the financial condition of their funds. Just like King George I closing the ports after the collapse of the South Sea Company to keep those responsible from absconding to the Continent, everyone was starting to point fingers and arrests were being made. At the close of June, the Dow was down more than 14 percent for the year. At this stage, it would have been easy for even the most financially literate to feel overwhelmed.

The firms that had failed prior to August 2008 were hardly pillars of Wall Street. Bear Stearns had failed and been acquired by JP Morgan Chase but Bear had been the runt among investment banks and was always seen as vulnerable in the face of a big mistake. New Century Financial was just twelve years old when it went belly-up but its failure was hardly surprising since it was at the epicenter of the whole misbegotten subprime mortgage craze. The twenty-year-old, California-based Independent National Mortgage Corporation—IndyMac for short despite having nothing to do with Indiana or Indianapolis—had operated on the fringes of the American financial system as a major issuer of subprime mortgages. It blew up in one of the biggest bank failures of all time on July 11. Nevertheless, the stock market bounced along with this news, as none of it was particularly unexpected. The Dow gained a fraction of 1 percent in July and nearly 1.5 percent in August.

But the companies that were pulled into the maelstrom beginning in September 2008 were the beating heart of Wall Street. If the measure of a financial catastrophe is the amount of history that comes undone, then that month in that year was without equal.

Nearly one home owner in four lost their homes to foreclosure during the Great Depression. Evicting families, of course, was devastating for them—but it didn't solve the problem for the banks or for the national economy either. Banks back then had limited capital and were forced to husband what remained so they weren't able to fill the gap and offer loans to home owners or potential home owners. The only entity with the resources to lend in that era was the federal government. In 1938, Congress established the Federal National Mortgage Association, soon nicknamed Fannie Mae. Banks would grant the sort of mortgages Fannie Mae wanted and Fannie Mae would in turn buy the mortgages from the bank, thus freeing up the banks' capital. The agency operated as an arm of the government until 1968 when it was spun out as a private company that was owned by shareholders but regulated by the federal government.

Fannie Mae served two masters for decades. The first was shareholders who expected a reasonable return on the capital they had invested. The second was the government which was still seen as Fannie's proverbial father. As if to emphasize this, Fannie and its sibling, Freddie Mac (the Federal Home Loan Mortgage Corporation), founded in 1970, were referred to as government-sponsored enterprises (GSEs). Since Fannie Mae was not just sponsored by the government but also regulated by it, the government was free to control the GSEs' business practices. Initially, it did so by implementing some common-sense and much-needed mortgage-issuing requirements—such as prohibiting discrimination on the basis of skin color. Then, in 1995, the government expanded its goals related to helping low- and moderate-income families everywhere—as well as some very-low-income families in certain areas—purchase homes.

In 2008, the GSEs owned or guaranteed nearly half the mortgages outstanding in the United States. In July, Fannie

Mae had $843 billion in mortgages on its books—a worrisome amount because Fannie had just $39 billion in capital so if the value of its portfolio of mortgages slid by just another 5 percent, Fannie Mae would become insolvent. This was no idle concern; the national home price index had already fallen more than 10 percent below its peak of 2006 and 9 percent of single-family homes had mortgages that were in foreclosure or were at least a month past due. In September 2008, Fannie Mae and Freddie Mac were crippled by falling housing prices. Enormous in size, barely solvent, and critically important to the economy, they found themselves beholden to the government. After markets closed on Friday, September 5, 2008, Treasury Secretary Henry "Hank" Paulson told the leadership of Fannie and Freddie that the federal government was assuming control. Although Paulson called it a "conservatorship," it was effectively a takeover.

During crashes and panics, investors like to see that the government or Federal Reserve is taking action—the lack of action on the part of President Herbert Hoover's government in the days and months following the stock market crash of October 1929 had exacerbated its impact many fold. Paulson had taken action, drastic action. The stock market rallied more than 2.5 percent when trading reopened on Monday. Regardless, this was the beginning of the end. The Dow gave back all of Monday's gain on Tuesday and most of the investors who had avoided information overload or the ostrich effect couldn't avoid either any longer.

Stocks dropped on Tuesday because word was out that Lehman's best hope for being saved had passed on making a deal. Lehman announced on Thursday what everyone knew: that it was looking to be acquired. The company was telling the world that it was merely illiquid—that is, the value of its assets was greater than all that it owed but those assets couldn't be sold easily. The world assumed, correctly, that Lehman was insolvent—that the value of its assets was *less* than all that it owed, regardless of their liquidity.

All that was left was for the body to hit the floor. That happened on Monday, September 15, 2008, when Lehman officially filed for bankruptcy.

Bank of America agreed to acquire Merrill Lynch for $50 billion on the same day. Although the price was a whopping 77 percent below the highest price Merrill had traded at in 2007, it was good for Merrill and spared the stock market from the

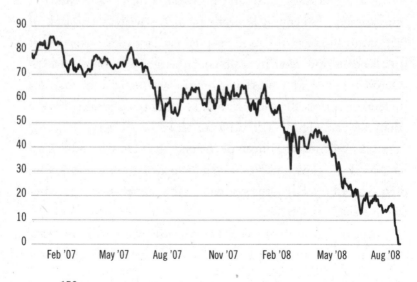

Lehman Brothers Stock Price, 2007 - 2008

agony of another colossal failure. The firm, unlikely to last another week, had been speeding head-long for a bankruptcy that would have been half-again as massive as Lehman's.

The S&P lost 4.7 percent that Monday, closing below 1,200 for the first time in nearly three years. Having declined 23.8 percent since its high in October 2007, it had now officially entered bear market territory. The day had seen two of the four remaining US investment banks disappear or be gobbled up. It had witnessed the largest bankruptcy filing in American history and had nearly seen one that was even larger. Investors were about to overreact.

The Federal Reserve was created in 1913 for just this sort of moment. Prior to the creation of the Fed, markets were left to lurch from panic, to crisis, to crash, with nobody other than private bankers such as J. P. Morgan left to lend what money and assistance they could. The Fed was always intended to be the lender of last resort and after failing at that in the 1930s, the leadership at the Fed has consistently understood the role the markets need it to play. In October 1987, the day after the most precipitous crash in Wall Street history, recently installed chairman Alan Greenspan became the archetype when he announced in a terse, businesslike memo that the Fed had money and was willing to lend all that was needed.

His successor, Ben Bernanke, had the benefit of hindsight but Bernanke understood better than anyone what the right approach to a financial crisis should be. One of the first academic papers he wrote, in 1983, argued that during the early years of the Great Depression, "some borrowers (especially households, farmers, and small firms) found credit to be expensive and difficult to obtain" and went on to argue that this was the reason the depression was so severe and lasted so long.

When the financial system started to come undone in 2007, Bernanke knew that the way to ease the strain was to cut interest rates. Accordingly, he cut one important short-term rate from 5.25 percent to nearly zero in only eighteen months. It may not be enough in the future, particularly if we never muster the will to allow interest rates to return to a normal level, but this is what investors should watch for during the tumult following, say, an invasion of Kuwait, or the bursting of the internet bubble, or a collapsing financial system, or a ravaging pandemic. If the Federal Reserve is aggressive in pushing interest rates lower to ease the strain, then they're doing the right thing.

Investors overreact during crashes and bear markets. Even when it seems like the world is coming to an end, meaning that overreaction would be nearly impossible, investors manage to do it. The financial world may have seemed like it was coming to an end in 2008 as Lehman Brothers went under and Merrill Lynch nearly did. The public shock in reaction to the collapse of Lehman Brothers was understandable. The US government had never simply washed its hands of a major financial institution that was in trouble. It had opened its checkbook and agreed to cover the first $29 billion in losses to make certain Bear Stearns was purchased in a civilized manner. Similarly, during the 1998 collapse of Long-Term Capital Management, a hedge fund headquartered in tony Greenwich, Connecticut, the US Treasury orchestrated a private-sector bailout involving a number of global investment banks. But this time, Treasury Secretary Paulson offered no such support to Lehman. That answered investors' question about what would happen to Lehman, it would go out of business, but it raised many more questions about the remaining banks. What would happen to the stock market if another one of them failed? Reaction spiraled into overreaction.

Most of us overreact to unexpected and dramatic events. It may be an evolutionary remnant of a time when an extreme reaction to a physical threat had little or no cost. That is no longer the case; an investor who overreacts and sells at the bottom experiences a real cost, the opportunity cost of not being invested when the market inevitably rallies. To fully unpack the mathematical irrationality of our responses in those moments, we need to take a trip across the Atlantic and back in time 250 years.

Thomas Bayes was an eighteenth-century British theologian and mathematician. Bayes spent most of his career as a Presbyterian minister who dabbled in mathematics. He published just a single paper regarding mathematics during his lifetime and even that paper had as much to do with theology as math; it was a defense of Isaac Newton's calculus against an attack by another theologian. But later in his life, Bayes turned his math skills to the study of probability, which was still poorly understood. He recognized that in trying to arrive at the correct solution to a problem, such as our modern problem of pricing the stock market correctly, each bit of new data should be incorporated appropriately in order to arrive at the most likely solution. His contribution was the mathematical formula that quantifies the probability of an event based on both the initial conditions and subsequent, relevant information. It can relentlessly nudge someone toward the right answer if they'll consistently incorporate new information and assign it the proper weight. While it's impossible to know the "correct" future value for a stock, Bayes's theorem can guide us to the correct reaction to news given all that has come before.

As an example, the S&P 500 has posted a gain in 56.3 percent in all weeks since 1962, so that is the base rate. But changes in interest rates exert a major influence on stock prices; stocks generally become less attractive as interest rates increase and more investors prove willing to take the sure thing and less inclined to take risks in the stock market. The conditional probability of the stock market gaining ground during any week declines as interest rates increase. Bayes's theorem tells us that the likelihood of any weekly increase in the S&P is only 55.2 percent if the ten-year Treasury rate increases at all. We know the base case, a gain in 56.3 percent of all calendar weeks, and we know the correct reaction to the news that interest rates have increased: a slight decrease in the likelihood of a weekly gain for the stock market. Bayes is nudging investors in the right direction. But investors don't care.

One reason is overreaction. While new data are vital, base case or long-term trends are more important than this morning's release of last quarter's earnings, or a marginal increase in interest rates, or even the collapse of an investment bank. Regardless, investors tend to focus on the most salient bit of information, even if it's merely anecdotal, and overreact to it. According to Bayes's theorem, new data should correct our course, but almost imperceptibly, whereas overreaction grabs the steering wheel and we veer into a ditch.

Complexity

A couple of centuries after Bayes, in June 1977, Daniel Kahneman and Amos Tversky were thinking about the problem of overreaction. They had been asked by the US military for advice about decision-making and in response wrote a paper that addressed "intuitive judgements and educated guesses." In it, they noted that humans have a tendency to give more consideration to more immediate information including breaking news or the largest price movements, and to give less consideration to data such as long-term averages. This same phenomenon applies to investors in the stock market and the result is overreaction, sometimes drastic overreaction, to today's news when it is viewed without regard to average returns of the past century. Kahneman and Tversky also pointed out that these errors of judgement are not random but "systematic"—in other words, stemming from deeply held bias. And, distressingly, for those who might think that trained professionals have had all the biases distilled out of their decision-making through training and education, Kahneman and Tversky showed that there is no difference in the decision-making process of the average recruit and the experts.

Maybe the best example of overreaction in the financial market is the tendency for both stock prices and the volatility of those prices to increase following the announcement that a company will split its stock. When a company splits its stock it issues new shares to existing shareholders in proportion to their existing holdings. If the company announces a two-for-one split, a shareholder with one hundred shares receives another hundred shares and has two hundred shares after the split, while an investor with five hundred shares owns a thousand shares after the split. The goal is to reduce the cost of each share in order to make a round lot of a hundred shares affordable to a larger universe of shareholders. If the total number of shares is doubled, but nothing else about the company changes, then the price of each share should be halved. A stock split should have no more impact on the total value of the company than changing a $20 bill for two $10 bills impacts the amount of money in your pocket. Yet one study found that stocks that announced a split gained 2 percentage points more than the market the next day. In another study, volatility in the price of the shares increased 30 percent after the split. Investors react, and overreact, to news that should have absolutely no effect on a company's total value.

The reaction to a stock split isn't the only overreaction an investor can see on the scale of a single day. Nearly all the trading that occurs each day is, in part, a function of overreaction to the tiniest tidbits of news. As John Maynard Keynes wrote in his 1936 book *The General Theory of Employment, Interest, and Money*, "Day-to-day fluctuations in the profits of existing investments, which are obviously of an ephemeral and nonsignificant character, tend to have an altogether excessive, and even an absurd, influence on the market." In other words, instantaneous price changes are overreactions to ephemeral fluctuations in a company's profitability. There is no good explanation for the amount of trading that takes place on stock exchanges every day so we're forced to see that trading through the lens of sensation seeking and overreaction.

Investors also overreact on longer time frames. One way to determine the value of a stock would be to sum the discounted cash flows it will generate in perpetuity, as I discussed in chapter

1. Despite having a time frame that might be described as "eternal," investors still overreact to things like a series of disappointing, short-term earnings reports and become overly pessimistic. In a seminal study, the Nobel Prize–winning economist Richard Thaler and Professor Werner F. M. De Bondt examined the full array of New York Stock Exchange common stocks from January 1926 to December 1982. They calculated each stock's performance over three-year periods then assembled two portfolios: Winner, made up of the best-performing stocks during the previous three-year period; and Loser, consisting of the poorest-performing stocks. Then they calculated the performance of each portfolio over the following three-year period.

The stocks in the Loser portfolio had been beaten down. They may have generated poor earnings or disappointed investors in some other way during the three-year formation phase when the stocks that would make up each portfolio were selected. Overreaction to that news, whatever it was, meant they had been beaten down too much; they had been pushed below their real value as they fell out of favor and investors threw in the towel. In much the same way, the stocks in the Winner portfolio had been bid up. They may have grown earnings or revenue faster than Wall Street had expected over the three years during the formation period. During that time, herding investors who were over-extrapolating gains drove their share prices above what was reasonable. How do we know investors had overreacted?

Because the Loser portfolios of what had been the worst performing stocks outperformed the broad market by an average of 19.6 percent during the three years following the formation of each portfolio. The Winner portfolios underperformed the broad market by 5.0 percent during that period. This means that the Loser portfolios did better than the Winner portfolios by an average of 24.6 percent.

Overreaction overcomes even the disposition effect which keeps us from selling moderate losers because we hope they'll bounce back. The very worst performers are most salient, the worst of the worst, and only when all hope for a rebound is finally lost, disposition gives way and overreaction kicks in.

The problem is not that investors overreact to a carefully curated analysis of all data. The problem is that they overreact to the most recent, most attention-grabbing data. Despite the power of tools such as Bayes's theorem, which can guide an investor toward understanding the logical magnitude of the reaction, we now know that the tools Bayes provides do not correspond to how individual investors actually respond to new news or data.

According to Kahneman and Tversky, this happens because people see extreme events, like one of the four remaining American investment banks going bankrupt, as more likely or even normal simply because they are recent and more retrievable. Investors grow to believe that these extreme events are representative of the entire range of possible outcomes merely because they are recent. Many of the biases that infect investors, especially during market turmoil, bleed into one another and resemble one another. Salience and availability are siblings. Herding and overreaction are cousins that push stock prices too low or too high. Prospect theory and the disposition effect bring about illogical differences in our approach to gains and losses. Hindsight bias fuels overconfidence, which leads to overtrading.

Complexity

The keys to successful investing include continuing to invest sensibly, even when times seem tough. And the way to do that is to understand the biases at work, inevitably pulling you in the wrong direction, and to account for those biases when making decisions.

When an investor is susceptible to the availability bias during market turmoil, they come to believe that the failure of one investment bank, the near failure of another, and a one-day 4.4 percent decline in the Dow are much closer to normal than they actually are. That means these investors come to believe that something much worse is relatively likely, when, in fact, it is extraordinarily unlikely. From the creation of the Dow Jones Industrial Average on May 26, 1896, through the end of 2021, the Dow has suffered a one-day percentage decline that is greater than 4.4 percent only 118 times. That's 0.35 percent of trading days or less than one per year. The average investor will think, "This happened yesterday, so it's normal." The logical investor will think, "This happened yesterday, but it's not representative of the long-term trend, so don't get pulled in."

Unfortunately, most investors get pulled in. They buy when the market is strong and they sell or don't invest at all when the market is weak—despite all their tough talk about how they'd love to see stocks pull back so they can buy good stocks at bargain prices. How extreme is the difference in investor activity during bull markets, when the market is strong, and bear markets, when it is weak? One gauge is net flows for equity mutual funds during those periods. From the beginning of 1960 to the end of 2020, the net monthly inflow averaged 0.20 percent of existing assets. This is new money invested less existing

159

investments that are sold. It is not a function of market fluctuations. During bull markets, this number increased to 0.23
percent of existing assets as investors *increased* their buying despite higher prices. If investors love to buy equity mutual funds
when they are relatively expensive, one might think they would
be ecstatic to buy them when they are on sale. But the average
monthly net inflows to equity mutual funds during bear markets over this sixty-one-year period was less than 0.01 percent.
Net inflows when prices are strong were more than twenty-five
times what they were when prices were weak. As a group, stock
market investors buy when prices are high. They stand on the
sidelines, doing nothing, when prices are low.

Investors who overreacted seemed to be vindicated in the
months after the collapse of Lehman Brothers. From the end of
September 2008 to March 9, 2009, when the stock market bottomed, the S&P 500 lost another 42 percent. For a time, those
who sold likely patted themselves on the back, and those who
didn't, regretted it.

But as studies of mutual fund flows and herding have
demonstrated, investors don't sell the top and buy the bottom.
Instead, they sell on the way down and keep selling right at the
bottom along with the herd. Then they don't buy back what
they've sold until after the market has rebounded.

Using that monthly data for US equity mutual funds, investors were net sellers of equity mutual funds through the last half
of 2008 and while they were small net buyers in January 2009,
they were again sellers in February and March 2009, just as the

market was hitting bottom. Some of these investors would have sold at the absolute low on March 9. But the important question might be, when did they get back in? We know that, in aggregate, they didn't buy back in that year because 2009 saw net selling of both domestic stock mutual funds and broad-based exchange-traded funds (ETFs).

When 2009 ended, the S&P 500 had gained more than 23 percent for the year. Thus, investors who sold in February or March had missed a monster rally. They had overreacted and joined the herd because sometimes the security promised by being part of the herd is more enticing than making money. Every adult who can remember doing something stupid as a teenager merely to be part of the group can recognize this.

Because the S&P gained 23 percent in 2009, it closed on December 31, 2009 just 6.5 percent below where it had closed on the day Lehman Brothers filed for bankruptcy; the whole fifteen months had nearly been a big roundtrip for the stock market.

Markets are extremely efficient even when they're not logical. Biases work against us because we're human. We're not trading very much if we're investing correctly so we can't learn through repetition. Investors absorb the wrong lessons because our biases masquerade as logic; disposition is seen as disciplining our greed, representativeness is dressed up as empirical evidence, herding appears to be taking advantage of momentum, and hindsight bias fools us.

One reason inexperienced investors do not learn is that they often do not know their past performance and can almost never correctly gauge the amount of risk they took compared with the broad market. A 2007 study asked 215 investors how their investments had performed during the past four years and then compared each answer to the actual performance of that investor's portfolio. According to the authors of the study, the correlation between these investors' self-reported performance and their actual performance was "not distinguishable from zero." In other words, these investors had no idea how their investments had actually performed during the previous four years. Not surprisingly, they tended to overestimate their performance with seven in ten investors surveyed thinking that they had enjoyed much better returns than they had. They also thought they had done better relative to other investors in the same way that some of us think we're more likely to have gifted children and less likely to be a victim of violent crime. Finally, these investors were even overconfident about how precisely they could estimate their previous performance, leaving them even more convinced that their guess was correct.

They are anything but. Only 61 percent even knew if they had made money or lost it, a number that suggests their guesses were barely better than random. The average investor overestimated their annual return by more than 11.6 percentage points. The one trait that seemed to ease this self-deception? Experience as an investor. Those who had more than five years' experience did better at estimating their previous returns. And as we know, understanding your performance is important to learning for everyone including meteorologists, handicappers, and investors.

While the best investors trade relatively infrequently and the worst investors trade most often, the process of executing trades did more to help these test subjects become better investors than the mere passage of time as an investor. One study from 2009 reviewed all trading by 1.3 million investors in Finland from 1995 to 2003. The results are striking; if a trader had the experience of placing an additional hundred trades during that period, or about one extra trade a month, their investment returns improved by about one-third of 1 percent a year while their tendency to give in to the disposition effect decreased. If the measure of experience the researchers used was replaced by years spent as an investor, the improvement disappeared. Time helps, but it only teaches certain lessons. *Doing* teaches other lessons.

How can we reconcile this outcome with the data that says overtrading hurts returns? It seems there's a middle ground, and a little trading—just enough to educate and engage us—is productive although not in the manner you'd expect. It's not that a little trading teaches us about different order types or how to analyze a company and its recent price action or the way in which the share price has bounced around. The study's authors write that instead, "This implies that the learning we document occurs primarily as investors learn about their ability." So, as investors learn about their own ability, including the degree to which they get pulled in by biases, they become better investors in a way that mere experience, as measured by years, can't match.

The stock market bottomed on March 9, 2009 with the S&P closing at 676.53—less than half of what it had been at its last high in 2007. It finished the year at 1,115.10 for a heartening recovery of 23.5 percent although it still hadn't regained 2008's loss. That happened in January 2013. It wasn't until March 2013 that the S&P hit another new all-time high. Investors who had been stampeded by the herd into selling in February and March 2009 would take years to recover, and then only after they were again invested in the market.

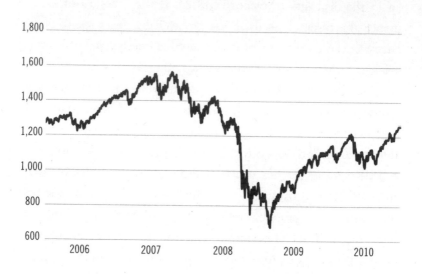

S&P 500 Index, 2006 - 2010

Probably the only Americans hit harder by what we came to call the Great Recession than the investors who sold their stock portfolios in February or March 2009 were the ten million Americans who lost their home to foreclosure. Any equity they had disappeared as home prices fell, then they were eaten up by the expense of foreclosure before they were essentially forced to sell their home at the very bottom, locking in that loss. Some had been herded into buying homes they couldn't afford. Many were abetted by mortgage lenders that had been herded into the subprime market by their competition. They were egged on by overconfidence that convinced them it would all work out in the end. Both the home buyers and lenders were further encouraged by the massive investment banks that considered mortgages just another cut of meat to be thrown into the grinder so that the sausage of tranched and rated mortgage-backed securities would come out the other end. And all of it was condoned by the rating companies such as Standard & Poor's and Moody's which were herded into competing for the intensely profitable business of rating these mortgage-backed securities so that institutional investors could buy them. A bubble is something many of them got fired for not participating in.

Heuristics, those shortcuts or rules of thumb we all use, seem particularly helpful when we're faced with a difficult problem or we're overloaded by information. That is the environment investors faced during 2008 and the first months of 2009. But heuristics were never supposed to provide the "right" answer and are instead supposed to provide a "good enough" answer that cuts through the information overload and peels away much of the difficulty. When combined with biases such as the tendency to buy stocks that have been in the news, or the overconfidence that leads to overtrading, or the hindsight bias that makes the past so vivid that it now seems it was always obvious, investors make mistakes. But after doing the analysis of the stock or exchange-traded fund or whatever the vehicle is, investors should stop for a moment and scrutinize themselves and their decision-making.

"The stock's price-to-earnings ratio is attractive, but am I interested in buying it only because it's been in the news?"

"Has the recent price action really been representative of the long-term price action?"

"Am I betting on a longshot only because I'm trying to get back to even or because I'm looking for the thrilling sensation of making a speculation?"

"Am I being overconfident in my ability to pick a stock that helps my portfolio?"

"Am I overreacting to some unexpected and dramatic event?"

"Is my estimation of the value of the stock a rigorous one devoid of emotion, or is it a function of anchoring?"

And so on.

Investing doesn't have to be hard but it can be difficult to do well if we're working against ourselves. Instead of examining balance sheets and stock charts, the best way to improve your investment results, particularly when you're anxious and markets are volatile, might be a little personal introspection.

A CHECKLIST FOR BETTER INVESTING

So now what?

Crashes and bear markets are inevitable. The longest period between bear markets is less than eleven years, from March 2009 to the start of the very brief but very ugly Covid-19-induced bear market that began in February 2020. The shortest is the period from September 1966 to November 1968. Every investor is almost certain to experience several bear markets.

The definition of a stock market crash is subjective so the number might be open for debate, but during that same period, our stock market has crashed at least three times. The one-day, 22 percent loss in October 1987, the more than 50 percent loss that spanned 2008 and 2009, and the one-month loss of more than 33 percent in 2020, certainly qualify.

The best thing to do in the midst of market turmoil like this is to take a deep breath and embrace an adage that's generally associated with the practice of medicine, "First, do no harm." Regardless of how long it's been since we've had some sort of gut-wrenching, insomnia-inducing market turmoil, one thing will remain constant: when it comes to your portfolio, the most dangerous element during the next stock market crash is likely to be you.

The first three chapters of this book have focused on the behavioral biases that make you so dangerous. Understanding them is the key to unlocking your best self as an investor. It's so important, in fact, that this chapter concludes with a checklist for the anxious investor—a refresher course on these psychological biases, to help you think through your own personal psychology and defeat the biases.

But before we get there, let's answer two fundamental questions because you need to have the answers in your toolkit to go with your newfound psychological edge.

The first: What is "normal" when it comes to the stock market?

And the second: When the market is behaving *abnormally*, which sorts of asset classes are likely to perform the best?

Until this point, we've had fun. We've learned how dumb the smartest man in the world could be. We've learned how smart some internet entrepreneurs could be in repackaging the mundane, like dog food, and selling their companies in IPOs the average guy scrambled to get in on. We've learned how a couple of twenty-three-year-olds can be simultaneously devious, ingenious, and felonious. And we've learned how investors are able to remain optimistic about the stock market in the face of a public meltdown of our housing and banking markets. The rest of what we're going to do doesn't have to be difficult. You'll be fighting against an arsenal of behavioral biases, but now that we understand some of them, we can develop the tools to over-come them.

WHAT IS NORMAL?

Just because it happened recently doesn't mean it is normal. In fact, if you can remember what happened—if it is readily avail-able in your memory—then it's probably not normal. Examples abound, and they usually begin "I'll never forget where I was the day . . ." Regardless of how sharp your memory might be, if whatever happened in the stock market was dramatic, then it was almost certainly not normal. What exactly is normal? Let's find out, because planning for the normal rather than the memorable is the best approach.

As noted in chapter 3, there were 33,825 trading days from Tuesday, May 26, 1896, the day the Dow was introduced, through Thursday, December 31, 2020. A slim majority of those days, 52.4 percent, saw the average close higher while it finished lower 47 percent of the time. An average of 1.5 days each year, 0.6 percent, saw the Dow finish unchanged. There is an average of just 13.5 more trading days with a gain than with a loss in a year. The average daily loss of 0.74 percent is slightly larger than the average daily gain of 0.72 percent. (One important note about all the Dow Jones Industrial Average and S&P 500 Index data in this section: it ignores dividends unless noted otherwise. This is standard because historical index data which accounts for dividends is a fairly recent innovation. The performance of the Dow and S&P would increase if we could account for dividends.)

It is normal for the stock market to fluctuate, for gains to be followed by losses, and for it to all seem random. In nearly every way it is random. Throughout our 124-year period, the stock market's performance on any one day has offered no clue as to its performance on the next. That is confounding for those who believe they see something else. It is particularly confounding for those who trade or invest based on momentum. It is expensive for those who follow the herd, extrapolating recent price action into future performance. How do we know that what happens today gives us no insight into what is likely to happen tomorrow, despite the apparent logic of such an assumption? We know because the correlation between one day's return in the Dow Jones Industrial Average and the next day's return is a statistically insignificant 0.014, or effectively zero. (This statistical measure of correlation between elements of one series and other elements from the same series separated by a constant time interval is called autocorrelation).

Correlation can range between 1.00 and -1.00. The higher the number the stronger the relationship as the two inputs move in the same direction. The lower the number the stronger the relationship as they move in opposite directions. A number close to zero means movement of the two inputs in unrelated.

Correlation of 0.014 means two inputs aren't connected at all. The same is true for monthly returns and yearly returns; the last time period's return tells us nothing about the next period's return just as the results of the previous spin of the roulette wheel, whether red or black, odd or even, tells us nothing about the likely outcome of the next spin. Extrapolating recent returns to future returns is a mistake. Buying into a bubble, overconfident that the trend will continue, is a great way to buy the top. You'll be part of the herd and that might make you feel comfortable but you'll also likely be worse off for it because even in the most runaway market in recent history, the Nasdaq Composite Index in 1999 which seemed to ooze momentum and correlation as it gained 85.6 percent for the year, the statistical measure of correlation from one day to the next is just 0.003, a miniscule number which means there was no correlation. Even when investors are certain they can see the momentum on the stock chart, it's a mirage.

With fewer than fourteen more profitable days than losing days in an average year, and a slightly larger average net loss, the difference between success and failure for investors would seem to rest on a knife's edge.

While there is no momentum, that doesn't mean stock prices don't tend to increase over time. But that increase is the work of compounding a few positive days each year rather than momentum.

The most important lesson the markets teach us is that the longer the holding period, the better the odds for investors. There were 1,491 months from the day the Dow was introduced to the last trading day in 2020. Of those months, 870, or 58.4 percent, ended with a gain while 621, or 41.6 percent, ended with a loss. Thus, in a typical year, seven months show a gain while five months generated a loss. Again, we see that the enormous growth in the Dow comes from a small number of time periods, just two months each year. The average monthly gain is slightly less than the average monthly loss: 3.8 percent to 3.9 percent respectively, so again the average loss is greater than the average gain.

During that 124-year period through 2020, the Dow posted a gain in 82 years, or 66.1 percent of the time, while 42 of those years, or 33.9 percent, brought losses. The odds have improved as the time frame gets longer, and, finally, the average gain, 19.1 percent, is greater than the average loss, 14.7 percent.

This is what normal looks like but it also highlights the critical element to remember when feeling anxious about your investments: time is important. Just 52.4 percent of trading days are profitable, but 58.4 percent of months are profitable; 66.1 percent of years are profitable; 73.0 percent of three-year periods

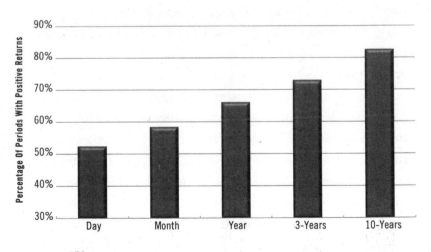

The Percentage of Profitable Periods Increases as the Timeframe Gets Longer

are profitable; and, of all the ten-year periods since the creation of the Dow, 82.6 percent are profitable with average gains of 107.2 percent and average losses of just 16.7 percent.

The odds of any time period being profitable improve as the time period gets longer. Even longer time frames that see a net loss tend to see less severe losses. During the three-year period from 2008 through 2010, which included the worst of the Great Recession—the most severe market pullback since the Great Depression—the Dow experienced a loss of 12.7 percent. But let's look at what happened on either side of that stretch. For the three years from 2005 through 2007, the Dow climbed by 23 percent, and from 2011 through 2013, it shot up 43.2 percent. The compound annual return over those nine years was 4.9 percent—not great, but not that far below the average considering that this stretch included a sickening crash. The best ten-year period was 1989 through 1998, when the Dow gained 323.4 percent, while the worst ten-year period, 1929 through 1938, saw a loss of 48.4 percent. Longer time frames help returns even when they include an ugly stretch.

Now a word about risk. Risk is the price you pay for additional return. It is the price you pay for getting that wonderful growth from stocks over time, and it means you'll occasionally be along for a gut-wrenching collapse. Another reason to take a breath in the middle of market chaos is to remind yourself of this. Risk usually works *for* you, helping to generate extra return. You don't have to be thrilled about taking on risk, but you can't completely avoid it and you shouldn't try. Why? Because the same $1 invested in risk-free US Treasury notes (while the price of a ten-year Treasury note will fluctuate, the investor who buys it when it is issued and holds it to maturity is effectively assuming zero risk) would have generated less than half the amount that the Dow did.

Another reason you shouldn't try to completely avoid risk is because, over time, stocks return more than they should. It's not just that stocks return more than bonds, they return even more than can be explained as fair compensation for the additional risk they bear over something that is risk free, like US Treasury notes. The Dow Jones Industrial Average has returned an average of 7.7 percent each year, ignoring dividends; US Treasury notes have returned an average of 5.1 percent annually during the same period. You would expect stocks to offer greater return, given that they also bear more risk but, in the long run, they return so much more than Treasury notes that the difference becomes inexplicable. The average annual equity risk premium—the difference between the annual return for the Dow and the annual return for ten-year Treasury notes—going back to 1896, is 2.6 percentage points. Adding dividends would increase that premium even further.

Why is the equity risk premium so large that, over its life, the Dow has returned an amount which is more than double the return that US Treasury notes generated? There are several theories, none of which is considered the last word, but one very plausible explanation has to do with the quirk of loss aversion, the greater displeasure felt upon a loss than the pleasure experienced after a gain of the same amount. Given this bias, it might be understandable when investors reduce the potential for losses by buying bonds (the impact of additional demand increases their price now and reduces their subsequent return) and shunning stocks (and similarly reducing their price now and increasing their subsequent return). This all makes sense once we acknowledge that loss aversion is real and it influences the way we deal with risk—including the risk inherent in investing. But as behavioral economist Shlomo Benartzi and Richard Thaler deduce in a 1993 research paper titled "Myopic Loss Aversion and the Equity Premium Puzzle," it also assumes that investors aren't taking advantage of those long time frames when the odds of a loss in the stock market become much smaller. Instead, they construct, and then periodically reconstruct, their portfolio as if their time frame—the period from now to when they plan on using their money—is much shorter than it actually is. Benartzi and Thaler dubbed this mismatch myopic loss aversion because we hate losses but we're shortsighted regarding our time frame.

The two examined the data in several different ways and were able to reverse engineer the time frame investors seem to focus on when constructing their portfolios, given the historical equity risk premium. "The answers we obtain," they write, "are all in the neighborhood of one year." That means investors as a group are focused on a one-year time frame with their investments, and this leads them to invest a smaller portion of their portfolio in stocks and leave more cash uninvested than they would otherwise. They do this despite the undeniable advantages of investing in stocks, the benefit of doing it for a much longer time period than one year, and without considering the point in time when they'll actually need the money.

Even a simpler look at stock and bond returns bears this out. The average annual dividend yield for the broad stock market has been approximately 4.1 percent since the launch of the

Dow. Add that to the Dow's average annual return of 7.7 percent (remember, this doesn't include dividends), and we have an average annual total return of about 11.8 percent. Recall that the average annual return for ten-year Treasury notes during the same period was 5.1 percent. If we remember the coin flip wager that MIT economist Paul Samuelson offered his colleague and then remember the research that shows the average person needs a potential return of between $200 and $250 (2.0 times to 2.5 times) to take the sort of bet Samuelson offered, the annual equity risk premium ratio of 2.31 makes perfect sense.

So now what? Don't create a portfolio or reweight your existing portfolio for a time frame other than the one that is appropriate. It's easy to understand how an investor might consider their annual return to be the jumping-off point for analysis and learning. Your brokerage statements will likely calculate it for you and it's an interval that comes frequently enough to seem impactful but infrequently enough to not seem prone to overtrading or sensation seeking. But your portfolio shouldn't focus on annual return; it should focus on the return from now until you'll use the money. For a thirty-year-old, it's certainly not when they're thirty-one. How can we do this?

Time is clearly one key to successful investing and not even higher returns will always make up for missed time. Ten years of compounding at 5 percent still offers a slightly greater return than five years at 10 percent (a gain of 62.9 percent versus 61.0 percent). Stay invested and keep investing with an understanding of your real time frame, not an artificial one you arrived at arbitrarily.

The urge to believe that some investors can time the market successfully is incredibly strong. It would seem that someone would have figured it out by now given all the effort and computing power spent on trying to beat the market. It appears that a couple of hedge funds might have solved the problem but they have strict capacity constraints meaning that their strategies work, but only with a limited amount of money. Furthermore, those strategies are blisteringly complex and expensive to implement. They also seem to take advantage of investors' behavioral biases rather than some underlying inefficiency in the stock market. The urge to believe that we, an individual investor, can beat the market is strong but it's fueled by overconfidence, hindsight bias, and our desire for it to be so. We can't beat the market; all we can do is make mistakes that ensure we won't even match its historical return.

The best results come from understanding what is normal and that results improve dramatically as the holding period increases. This helps investors understand what to do - rely on the normal, keep investing, and plan on an extended holding period, as well as what not to do meaning don't invest money you're certain to need within the next year in the stock market if a 20 percent loss would be unbearably painful.

Given that stocks earn more than they should for the amount of risk investors assume, normal does not mean certain, but it does get the odds on your side.

WHAT WORKS?

Diversification is the only free lunch on Wall Street. Diversification doesn't just reduce risk, it actually increases returns over time. However, as illogical as it may seem, many investors would rather pay their own way.

We have seen already how much more the Dow Jones Industrial Average returned than Treasury notes did, and that the difference is a result of the short-term safety provided by Treasury notes. So, it would seem that adding the slower-growing Treasury notes to a portfolio that mimicked the Dow would only drag it down. But together the two generate even better returns than the Dow alone. A dollar invested in a portfolio that is made up of 70 percent the Dow and 30 percent US Treasury notes, from the creation of the Dow to the end of 2020, would have grown to $995.37. What matters here is the diversification, not the precise ratio; a portfolio that was 60 percent the Dow and 40 percent US Treasury notes would have grown to $991.78.

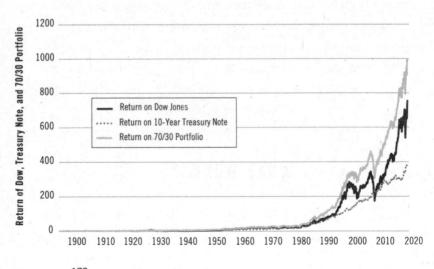

Diversification is Key: Dow Jones, 100-Year Treasure, and a 70/30 Portfolio

A Checklist for Better Investing

	Dow Jones Industrial AVerage	S&P 500 Index	Russell 2000 Index	10-Year Treasury Notes	70%Dow Jones, 30% Treasury Notes	Housing Prices
Compound Annual Return Since 1988	8.7%	8.6%	8.8%	6.6%	8.4%	3.8%
Annualized Risk	14.4%	14.5%	19.1%	6.1%	9.9%	2.2%
Average Annual Sharpe Ratio	.76	.87	.59	.68	.88	.81

Note: Sharpe Ratio is a measure of risk-adjusted return. It measures how much return is generated for each unit of risk. Thus, higher is better.

Diversification doesn't just generate better returns, it also decreases risk. The variability of the Dow Jones Industrial Average alone was 65 percent greater than that of the portfolio that is 60 percent stocks and 40 percent US Treasury notes. Academics consider this variability to be the best measure of risk.

ASSET CLASSES AND BEAR MARKETS

During bear markets and, more generally, times of market turbulence, one question always comes to mind: Do some assets perform better than others?

We have good data for a broad range of asset classes for the four most recent bear markets, beginning with the short and mild one that occurred in the summer of 1990, the much longer one that began in March 2000, the horrible one that commenced in October 2007 as the housing bubble crashed, and the vicious but brief one that gripped the country with the arrival of the coronavirus in February 2020. The range of asset classes I'll be looking at are: (1) the United States' biggest companies, as expressed by the Dow Jones Industrial Average; (2) the broader group of large-capitalization stocks that make up the S&P 500 index; (3) the small capitalization stocks that make up the Russell 2000 index which includes most of the listed companies which fall outside the largest one thousand; (4) ten-year Treasury notes; and (5) real estate as expressed by the S&P/Case-Shiller US National Home Price index. Investing in real estate generally involves headaches that these other classes do not (not everyone wants to be a landlord!), but since their home is the single largest asset most Americans own, I include real estate in the analysis. We'll investigate each of these

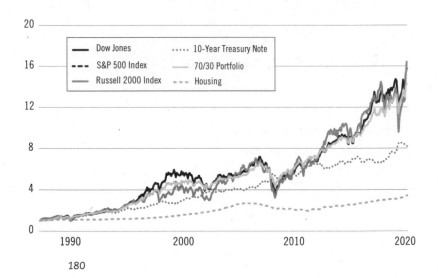

Major Asset Classes, 1998 - 2020

five categories leading up to and during the four recent bear markets mentioned above.

You may be wondering about other asset classes that are both exotic and illiquid—stuff like venture capital funds and hedge funds. Those vehicles may be important for an institution with a huge portfolio and the need to get exposure outside mainstream investments. That is almost never going to be an individual investor. We've all heard about famous athletes and entertainers who made a bunch of money and then went broke and the story usually includes both profligate spending and strange, illiquid, high-cost investments. The story never includes disciplined investing in a mainstream portfolio made up of high-quality stocks, low-cost exchange-traded funds that track the broad market, and diversifying bonds. Let's take a lesson from that.

1990

Americans were caught off guard when Iraqi dictator Saddam Hussein's army invaded neighboring Kuwait in August 1990. They had been tallying up their "peace dividend"—the money they would save on defense spending now that the Soviet Union was in the process of collapsing. The United States had won the Cold War without firing a shot and many Americans thought much of the money our federal government had been pouring into national defense—more than $300 billion in 1988 alone— would stay in their pockets in the new decade. Then on August 2, 1990, a hundred thousand men making up four divisions of the Iraqi military, said to be the world's fourth largest, poured over the southern border into Kuwait, a tiny country with fewer than twenty thousand soldiers on active duty.

Iraq had been complaining for months that Kuwait was stealing Iraqi oil and it now seemed Iraq was preparing to redress its grievance. The price for crude oil in the United States jumped from barely $20 a barrel in July to $40 in September once it became obvious that Hussein wasn't going to withdraw. President George H. W. Bush ordered a defensive military operation called Desert Shield which was intended to ensure that Iraq didn't attempt to invade Saudi Arabia. The result of the shock was a brief bear market that began in July and lasted just three months.

The Dow had peaked in the middle of July 1990 and meandered for the rest of the month in a way that is familiar to anyone who watches the stock market in the middle of summer. But when news of the invasion broke, the Dow fell 6.3 percent over the next three days. By October, it was down 21 percent. The mega-capitalization stocks in the Dow are often said to be the first ones sold by institutional investors because it is assumed they offer the most liquidity. As would be expected, the S&P 500 behaved similarly, although, at its lowest point, the S&P was down just 19.9 percent.

On January 16, 1991, after months of diplomacy failed to bring Hussein to heel, the US mission in the Middle East changed from Desert Shield to Desert Storm. The Iraqi army couldn't endure thirty-eight days of relentless US air power regardless of where its military ranked in size. On February 28, Iraq withdrew its military from Kuwait, all but bringing the war to an end. The formal end came on April 7 when Iraq meekly accepted the unforgiving terms of a UN Security Council resolution demanding that Hussein give up all weapons of mass destruction as well as repay Kuwait for damages incurred during its seven-month occupation. As fears of a protracted war and indiscriminate use of chemical weapons faded, the Dow gained back all it had lost in just nine months; the S&P gained back its own losses in seven months.

The Russell 2000 index of small-capitalization stocks had the toughest time during the short bear market in 1990. It actually peaked in October 1989 and tailed off slightly until July, when it really broke down along with all the other equity markets. From top to bottom, the Russell 2000 lost 34.3 percent during its own bear market from October 1989 to October 1991. Small-capitalization stocks like the ones in the Russell 2000 index are thought to be impacted by different factors than the Dow and S&P. They have less exposure to international trade but are also thought to be less able to handle a prolonged downturn. That reduced exposure to trade didn't help in 1990, which demonstrates that what we think we know about how any particular asset is going to respond to any particular event is largely rubbish. Small-cap stocks can provide diversification in a portfolio, but if you buy only the ones that grab your attention, they're not helping.

The real advantage of diversification is seen in the performance of the ten-year Treasury note, which we use as a proxy for bonds in general during this period. During the bear market for the Dow and S&P, the ten-year Treasury gained 4.7 percent as investors searched for a safe haven for their capital. This is how diversification works; while the value of a diversified portfolio dropped, it dropped less than it might have thanks to the contribution from

Treasury notes. The Dow itself has grown so much over time despite a net of just 13.5 positive days in a year by gaining, falling back slightly to a higher level than it was at previously, and building from there. Diversification into some fixed-income vehicle like Treasury notes just does that in an additional dimension.

Their home is often the largest asset an investor owns. It shouldn't be viewed as an investment in the same sense as stocks and bonds—the fact that you have to have some place to live is one simple reason why, and the fact that homes tend to be illiquid is another—but it is important for investors nonetheless. Housing prices topped out in July 1990 and bottomed in March 1991 as the outcome of the war became certain and Iraq agreed to the terms of a cease fire. Nationwide, housing prices had fallen by 3.1 percent but they recovered by July 1993.

There are a number of lessons an investor can learn from the brief and minor bear market in 1990. First, there's no telling what's going to spark the sell-off and there's no assurance you're going to get any warning. Your portfolio needs to be diversified to handle this sort of thing before it happens. The second is that diversification works. The Dow Jones Industrial Average lost 21.2 percent from the high to the low during the bear market that began in July 1990 and ended in October 1990. A portfolio that had been simply diversified with 70 percent Dow Jones Industrial Average and 30 percent Treasury notes would have lost less than 15 percent during that time, but more importantly, it would have regained it all two months sooner than something that was invested completely in stocks. The third lesson is the value of doing no harm. Investors would have been rightly concerned about many things once they heard the news of the invasion and the United States' likely intervention. They may have been uneasy when oil prices doubled, which is a more prosaic worry. But those who overreacted and ignored long-term trends for the more mentally available news would regret it just a few months later. And who's to know how high a price they finally paid when they got back in.

Major Asset Classes, November 1990 - 1991

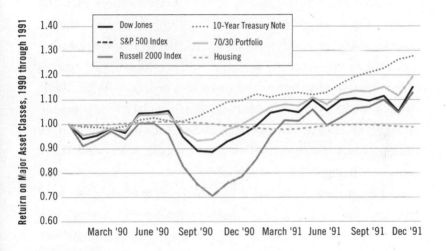

2000

The bear market that started in 2000 was initially our own fault. Stocks in general, and internet stocks in particular, rallied to unsustainable levels. The price-to-earnings ratio for the S&P rose above 32 in 1999, its highest level ever to that point. The P/E ratio for the Nasdaq Composite, with all its internet stocks, was even more obscene as herders bought shares in those phantastic companies. When stocks started coming back to earth, the gentle drop in prices turned into a cascade.

The Dow peaked in January 2000, two months earlier than the Nasdaq and the S&P 500. Two and a half years later, the Dow had lost 37.8 percent of its value because the initial decline gained speed after the sucker punch of 9/11.

The broader-based S&P 500 peaked in March 2000, a few days after the Nasdaq, and it fell 49.1 percent, more than the Dow, due to its greater exposure to technology and internet stocks. Internet stocks were added to the S&P 500 beginning in 1998 and they usually replaced "old economy" stocks to reflect the changing face of the American economy. When AOL joined the S&P 500 in December 1998, it replaced the company formerly known as Woolworth's. When Yahoo joined the index a year later, it replaced Laidlaw Inc., a decidedly low-tech operator of intercity buses and school buses.

The Russell 2000 index lost 46 percent during the bear market that started in 2000 but it bounced back more quickly; it made a new all-time high in May 2004 and was trading above that level by the end of the year. In contrast, the S&P didn't regain its 2000 high until May 2007, and, at that point, the Russell 2000 index was 37 percent above the high it had reached in 2000. The lesson is that diversification works, and while we've stuck with the Dow Jones Industrial Average and ten-year Treasury notes for simplicity's sake, the best diversification schemes are the ones that focus on the entire US stock market, not just the largest, most salient names like the ones in the Dow.

Interestingly, housing prices never fell during the 2000

bear market for stocks; they actually rose 7.2 percent from March 2000 to the end of the year as the Federal Reserve engineered lower interest rates to help the broad economy deal with the impact of the internet crash. This made mortgages more affordable. It is not unusual for housing prices to buck the trend and remain strong even when stocks are under pressure.

Investors are looking for safety during bear markets like the one that started in 2000 and they usually turn to something like Treasury notes. From January 2000, when the Dow peaked, to October 2002, when it bottomed, an investment in ten-year Treasury notes would have returned 39.3 percent as the Federal Reserve slashed interest rates in response to everything that had happened and as borrowing slowed. The decline in interest rates would increase the value of Treasury notes. That's why diversification works.

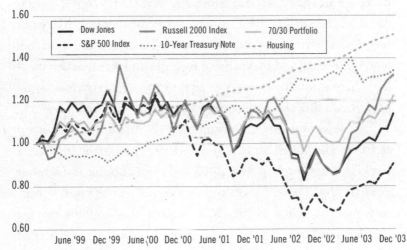

Major Asset Classes, 1999 - 2003

2007

The simple fact that banks around the world were warning that a slight downtick in housing prices was playing havoc with their profitability might seem to be all an investor needed to know to exit the stock market in the summer of 2007. It clearly wasn't. A few hedge fund managers got both wealthy and famous for betting against the housing market, but they haven't been able to replicate those results. It all shows that as obvious as it seems later, it's impossible to know what the stock market is going to do other than fluctuate in the short term and appreciate in the long term. The way to ease your anxiety during times of stress is to recognize this.

The housing market predictably got pummeled during its own bear market. It fell by 27.4 percent after peaking in July 2006 and bottomed in February 2012. That's an incredible move for an asset that has historically been 85 percent less volatile than the stock market. Much of that difference is likely the result of sensation seeking and overreaction in a stock market where it is easy and inexpensive to trade and a real estate market where it would never occur to most people to trade actively because it's difficult and expensive.

As we've discussed, housing took the stock market with it as banks got pulled under. The S&P 500 had barely managed to make a new high in May 2007 and then another in October after the 2000 bear market and recovery. Over the next seventeen months, it would lose 56.8 percent in a horrible market that left nowhere to hide and is eclipsed only by the disaster of the 1930s. The S&P was eventually able to make a new all-time high in March 2013, more than five years after the previous top, but that happened only because the Federal Reserve had learned its lesson and slashed interest rates when the crisis unfolded and kept short-term interest rates at essentially zero for seven years. With no return to be had in holding bonds or putting money in a bank account, investors don't have many choices. Eventually, they held their collective nose and started buying stocks again. It was the right move, as it usually is, particularly when interest rates are low and the expected holding period is long.

The Dow followed a similar path; it peaked on the same day as the S&P and bottomed on the same day seventeen months later. However, the Dow lost a bit less than the S&P, 53.8 percent, but that wouldn't have made much difference to investors who were weary of losses.

The Russell 2000 index of small-capitalization stocks again peaked before the other indexes. The Russell 2000 topped out in August 2007 and it fell more, bottoming out on the same day as the Dow and S&P but with a loss of 59.9 percent. The smaller stocks that make up the Russell 2000 index are like skirt lengths and punk-rock lyrics. They go in and out of fashion as overconfident investors begin to believe they know what will impact particular stocks and fool themselves about the precision with which they know it. By 2009, the Russell 2000 had done slightly worse than the S&P. In the bear market that began in 2000, it had done slightly better. Clearly, what matters more than the equity index represented is limiting the damage your behavioral biases can do.

Diversification is like insurance: you have to get it before you need it. Bond prices had surged during the dot-com bear market and that salvaged the results for many diversified investors. But bond prices hadn't managed to get back to a more normal, lower level when the housing market melted down. That was a major reason mortgage-backed securities were so popular; they paid a little more in interest than Treasury notes. But Treasury notes still helped diversified investors. From the start of the bear market in stocks to its end, ten-year Treasury notes returned 25.8 percent. A 70/30 portfolio took a beating, as would be expected, but during the period that saw the Dow losing 53.8 percent, the diversified portfolio would have lost just 33.8 percent and would have recovered more quickly. The Dow didn't make a new high until March 2013. This diversified portfolio would have recovered by February 2011, more than two years before the Dow.

Major Asset Classes, 2007 - 2009

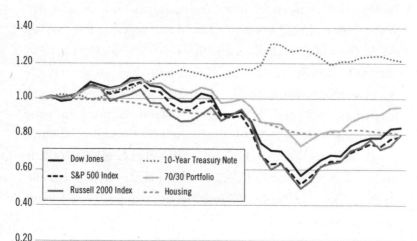

2020

If the bear market that Saddam Hussein kicked off in 1990 doesn't convince investors that it's impossible to see disaster coming, the Covid-19 crash in 2020 should do the trick. The public health disaster unfolded with astonishing quickness. The first death in China was reported on January 11. Cases were reported in the United States nine days later and just three days after that the entire Chinese city of Wuhan, home to more than eleven million people, was quarantined by the Chinese government. The World Health Organization declared a public health emergency on January 30. But it happened so fast—the disease the virus causes wasn't even named until February 11—that investors kept buying. The very next day, February 12, the Dow made another new all-time closing high of 29,551.42. That was the top. The bottom came forty days later when the Dow closed at 18,591.93, a loss of 37 percent.

The S&P 500 faced similar selling pressure. Its closing high came a week later than the one for the Dow but the result was the same. By the time the S&P bottomed on March 23 it had lost 33.9 percent, a little less than the Dow. The S&P also gained back its ground more quickly. It made another new all-time high on August 18, six months after its previous high; the whole thing had been a nauseating six-month round-trip. A diversified portfolio of 70 percent stocks and 30 percent Treasury notes made it back a month faster in part, because its maximum loss was just 12.6 percent. For those who did no harm, diversification ended up once again being the key.

The Russell 2000 index of small-capitalization stocks had peaked earlier then the Dow and the S&P once again. The Russell topped out at 1,705.22 on January 16. When it bottomed on March 23—all the major stock indexes bottomed on the same day—it had lost 41.2 percent. Many thought that the smaller companies in the Russell 2000 index would have a tougher time surviving whatever was coming next.

The Federal Reserve stepped up in the face of a public health emergency that was triggering a financial crisis. In the span of two months, it cut its key interest rate from 1.5 percent to zero, indicating that the lender of last resort was ready to help. Not surprisingly, when interest rates are falling and financial markets are in turmoil, investors reach for the safest thing they can find, US Treasury notes. The price of the ten-year Treasury note rose 4.8 percent from the end of January 2020 to March 23, 2020, the day the stock market hit bottom.

One unexpected aspect of the March 2020 bear market was the desire to quarantine in a nicer home. Housing prices rose 9.9 percent from February 2020 to the end of that year. It was the greatest ten-month increase in housing prices since a brief bounce in 2013. Otherwise, you would have to go back to the heart of the housing bubble in 2005 to find a bigger increase in housing prices.

Some would later swear they had seen the break coming. Many of those people would also swear they had seen the rebound coming. From that low on February 12, the Dow would gain 27.6 percent in the next forty days and would get all the way back by the middle of November.

. . .

Some readers will be disappointed I haven't offered a silver bullet to guarantee investing success. They'll be looking for answers to all their questions.

Major Asset Classes, 2020

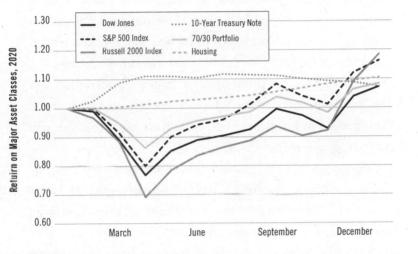

I hope that I've provided answers to the most important questions that we're capable of answering. If the question is "What is the silver bullet? What stock or fund or asset class is going to do best during the next twelve months?" then you've asked a question that can't be answered. Nobody can answer those questions accurately and the only ones who believe they can are the overconfident ones who don't understand anyway.

The strategy is to ask yourself questions such as "Why do I want to do that, and is it because of the behavioral biases we've examined?"

We have examined the behavioral biases in context related to actual market action. The following section will look at each of them, including some we haven't discussed yet, in a more conversational and inquisitive tone that will help readers understand if they reflect their own behavior. By looking at the biases in this manner, and providing some additional elements to think about, we'll help change behaviors. This interactive approach should make it easier to understand a bias when it threatens to derail your investment process and hurt investment returns.

To the degree that there's a silver bullet, it's boring. Invest. Keep investing. Stay invested. Use the tools described to avoid running afoul of behavioral quirks because none of them will help your long-term results. Diversify.

The interesting thing about this approach is that it eliminates all the day-to-day time wasting, hand wringing, and anxiety generated by always focusing on the stock market, talking about it with everyone, overtrading, and overthinking. You're going to rely on the proceeds of your investments at some point. It is important to get it right. Investors who are anxious recognize that investing is important to their future. They also realize that anxiety is likely to make things worse if it drives them to give in to their weaknesses and stop investing. Be anxious, because investing is important. Then be calmed by understanding the right path and recognizing that following it means less of the manic activity that is counterproductive. Be calmed by doing not just the right thing, but the best thing.

THE BIASES, HOW THEY WILL LEAD YOU ASTRAY AND THE TOOLS TO AVOID THAT

We've examined several of the behavioral biases that are going to hurt your investment returns and generate anxiety when markets are falling. We looked at them in the context of actual bubbles and bear markets although we have to fight against them even when markets are placid. The following checklist examines them in a more neutral setting but will also help you ask yourself important questions about when you might fall prey to them and what you can do to prevent or mitigate the damage.

Everyone exhibits some of these because we're all human. But good investors learn to identify them in their natural setting, before they cost money. Mediocre investors learn to identify them only in retrospect, but, still, those who do so become better investors. Bad investors are bad because of the biases themselves; they are overconfident and don't think they need to improve. They think that herding and disposition are legitimate investment strategies. They practice myopic loss aversion by setting up a portfolio for a one-year time frame even though they won't use the money for decades.

Examine these biases now, when you don't feel the pressure to trade or make changes in your portfolio. The clear light of morning is the time to ask yourself the questions posed here: Do you do this? When? Why? Then revisit this checklist before you make important financial decisions or readjust your portfolio. Ideally, you'll revisit this checklist regularly because as you grow, some of the biases will become less important but others may become more important. After revisiting, you'll become a more introspective investor, meaning you'll become a better investor.

STATUS QUO BIAS

Status quo bias is the irrational tendency to prefer choices that maintain the status quo even when other choices would leave us better off. This tendency has implications for your choice of a health care plan during your employer's annual open enrollment period and for marketers of sugary soft drinks who may forget that customers hate change even more than they like a tastier soda.

It's easy to believe that status quo bias is a matter of laziness, but for many people it's a matter of not knowing where to start and not having a process for analyzing, understanding, and comparing the alternatives. It seems that the comparison is never straightforward; one insurance plan will have a slightly different deductible or out-of-pocket maximum and while each difference should have some quantifiable, actuarially understandable effect on the cost of the insurance, it's confusing and intimidating. Is this you? Are you willing to do the work if you know what the work is? We'll discuss how to make the work worthwhile, at least as it applies to your investments.

One of the first academic tests of the phenomenon of status quo bias in finance asked college students how they would invest a hypothetical windfall they had inherited recently from a hypothetical great-uncle. They were given four alternatives: two were different investments in the stock market, one was riskless Treasury bills, and the last was tax-free municipal bonds. In one version of the test, the four alternatives were presented on an equal footing and as new suggestions. In a second version, different groups saw different alternatives as the status quo.

Regardless of which of the four alternatives was framed as the status quo, the test subjects always preferred the status quo option. When tax-free municipal bonds were the status quo option it was selected by 47 percent of the students, even though tax-free municipal bonds are almost never going to be the right investment choice for a college student. But the tendency to stick with the status quo runs deep, particularly when the mental cost of researching other alternatives is high or if the differences between the alternatives are confusing—as they can be when investing money inherited from a great-uncle or comparing health care plans. If you think status quo bias is strong when the only thing a consumer has to do is pick a brand of soda, imagine how difficult it is to overcome when faced with thousands of investment alternatives in a tumbling stock market.

As an investor, status quo bias will weigh on you, making it more difficult to implement positive changes such as rebalancing your portfolio so that it is properly diversified or harvesting tax losses. Tied to this weight will be prospect theory which tells us that people are less interested in saving money or changing their portfolio to generate better returns than they are in avoiding a penalty. We can take advantage of that as motivation for doing the work we need to do.

Since investors' minds are the problem, let's learn to trick your mind. What number equals 5 percent of your investment portfolio? It is reasonable to believe that number is the total that is at stake each year when we take advantage of diversification, avoid disposition, work through information overload, and avoid the herd. For a portfolio that totals $100,000, the fee you're paying yourself is $5,000 so imagine that pile of cash. By spending an hour making certain your portfolio is diversified in low-cost vehicles that avoid the herd, you'll avoiding paying a $5,000 surcharge for being inert or lazy or biased.

DISPOSITION EFFECT

While none of the behavioral biases we've discussed improve long-term investment returns, it would seem that the disposition effect would be the most likely. As you now know, the disposition effect is the human tendency to defer regret by holding on to losers and to spark the pleasurable swirl of chemicals in our brain by selling winners. This might seem to be a disciplined reaction that avoids the negative impact of greed but it doesn't work. As Professor Terrance Odean has demonstrated, the disposition effect leads you to sell stocks that outperform the ones you replace them with. Investors who give in are usually left with a portfolio full of losers that looks like a collection from the Island of Misfit Toys.

Disposition is so difficult to avoid because it works through brain chemistry and encompasses other behavioral issues, including prospect theory, regret aversion, and self-control. Disposition effect will push you to sell your winners, while herding and over-extrapolating recent results will push you to use those proceeds to buy whatever has done best in the past, with no regard for its future prospects.

But are you giving in to disposition because you hate to be wrong? That's natural, but it also ignores the fact that if your investment has lost ground then you're *already* wrong; realizing your loss doesn't make you any more wrong. In fact, realizing your loss and moving on to another investment is what is likely to make you less wrong. The most powerful element in investing is time and you're wasting it by sticking with an investment that isn't working. This is more likely if you're picking individual stocks that might move independently of each other or the broad market.

The tool here is to structure your portfolio differently. Stick with broad-based exchange-traded funds that provide both diversification in a single security and incredibly low cost, rather than buying individual stocks. Then remember that you're going to stay invested. You're not going to fall for the idea that what is happening right now, no matter how horrible it seems, is normal, because that will lead you to sell at the bottom. Instead, you are going to invest—and stay invested—for what is normal, not most memorable. If you're going to stay invested in broad based, low-cost exchange-traded funds, you're not likely to be susceptible to disposition. After all, selling to realize a gain doesn't make much sense. What else are you going to buy? Another broad-based, low-cost ETF? There's no point in selling then. That is the first step when we say, "Do no harm."

How do we reconcile two seemingly contradictory notions: the implication in the disposition effect that we should be selling our losers rather than our winners, and the quantitative research indicating that those losers are often underwater because of overreaction to the downside and are set to outperform the stocks that have done best over the previous three years?

This is a conundrum. But remember that the stocks De Bondt and Thaler picked for their Loser portfolio were the very worst performers during the formation period. In fact, they were the worst of the worst and there were few of them. They were in the Loser portfolio because investors had overreacted and pushed them below their fundamental value. The losers in your portfolio, the ones you hang on to, are more likely to come from the broad swath of stocks that are mediocre losers and haven't yet experienced the overreaction that would drive them even lower. They're not the worst of the worst, but they're not making you any money either. Avoiding individual stocks and focusing instead on broad-based asset classes is one way to reduce the dissonance between these two competing impressions.

HINDSIGHT BIAS

Hindsight bias isn't a matter of saying, "It all makes so much sense now, how could I not have seen it coming" and is instead fooling ourselves into thinking that we did see it coming because it is all so obvious now. We're wrong when we fall for it.

Think back to the Great Recession or the short bear market from March 2020. Do you fool yourself into thinking it was so obvious back then just because it is so vivid and memorable now? The problem is not just that you are fooling yourself about the past. It is that in fooling yourself about the past, you are becoming overconfident about your ability in the future. Professor Shiller's survey of investors following the 1987 stock market crash demonstrated that many had convinced themselves they had seen the crash coming because *in retrospect* it all made so much sense. The market had gained more than 40 percent for the year by August 1987 and many thought that was not sustainable, while only the most overconfident extrapolated the gains. The market had weakened some by October and the week before the crash was extremely volatile; the Dow lost 108.35 points on Friday, October 16, the largest-ever point loss then. Looking back, the 22 percent loss on October 19, Black Monday, seems obvious. The narrative was so vivid because it was so dramatic and emotional, so much so that many people even experienced a physical reaction. In Shiller's survey, 43.1 percent of the institutional investors who responded reported difficulty concentrating, sweaty palms, tightness in the chest, irritability, and/or a rapid pulse during or just after the crash.

Dangerously, hindsight bias convinced many investors in 1987 that they could see the next crash coming. But it also convinced them they could buy the next bottom because stocks had rallied from there. While the morning of October 20, the day following the crash, looked ugly at one point, that was the bottom. By the time Shiller's respondents received the survey and were filling it out, the Dow had recovered about 40 percent of Monday's loss. Anyone who bought late on the nineteenth was a hero. About 3 percent of Shiller's individual investors actually bought stocks on October 19. Nearly 30 percent said they had done so when asked a few days later, crediting "intuition" or a "gut feeling" that the market was going to bounce back.

One odd facet of overconfidence is not just that it convinces us that we're better than we are, but also that we can see the future with more precision than we really can. It's not just investors believing they can sell near the top or buy close to the bottom, but also that they can sell at the absolute top or buy at the very bottom. That level of overconfidence is insane.

Another reason overconfidence born of hindsight bias is dangerous is that the drivers of what comes next aren't objective and, in the case of the stock market, investors may not even agree on what subjective catalysts will be at work. More than two-thirds of the individual investors in Shiller's 1987 survey thought the crash was a function of "investor psychology" rather than fundamentals such as "profits or interest rates." That means the overconfident don't have to gauge the Bayesian reaction to earnings releases or interest rate changes but instead have to read other investors' minds. Good luck with that.

Hindsight bias will fool you into taking too much risk, feeling confident that you'll decode the narrative in real time or read investors' minds and get out of the market at the top or jump into the market at the bottom.

The tool for defeating hindsight bias is to remember how those investors were so certain they had seen the 1987 crash and subsequent rebound coming when objective analysis of their actual trading activity proved the opposite. You'll remember that it was well after the first public announcements in 2007 about huge global banks being in trouble because of mortgage-backed securities that our stock market posted a new all-time high. Nobody knew anything about how stocks would react. You'll also remember that high point came more than two months *after* the

Bear Stearns hedge funds declared bankruptcy. Investors didn't know what to think of that. And you'll remember that it came four days after Merrill Lynch announced a $5.5 billion loss due to mortgage-backed securities. That news was dismissed.

So, one tool is to ask yourself what the stock market will do next week. If hindsight bias convinces us that we should be able to divine what will happen in the future, asking ourselves what will happen next week should disabuse us of that notion. There's no way to know what will happen next week and when we look forward instead of backward, our overconfidence should evaporate, particularly if we revisit our prediction and grade ourselves on its accuracy.

Another tool is to remember that there is no momentum from day to day, month to month, or even year to year. There's no correlation between one period's returns and the next period's. That means it is impossible, no matter how fervently your brain "misremembers" doing so, to pick the top or know that stocks are going to fall.

OVERCONFIDENCE

Investing successfully has never been more important given the demise of the traditional pension. That change shifted the risk for generating investment results from your employer to you. With investing now critical, it seems odd that anyone could be overly confident. There are thousands of stocks an investor can buy. There are even more funds than stocks and there are more opaque specialty products, such as annuities, than funds. There are competing strategies and diversification schemes. Add the jargon and occasional unnecessary complexity, and the idea that anyone can be overconfident about investing is surprising.

Overconfidence among investors operates on many levels. It causes them to extrapolate past trends even though there's no correlation between what happened today and what is going to happen tomorrow. If you do this, remember that there is no follow-through and that past trends are just that—past. Ignoring this tends to inflate bubbles as investors assume there will always be a greater fool willing to pay even more.

Overconfident investors are more likely to invest using borrowed money, or "margin." Professor Odean of the University of California has found that margin investors tend to trade more, speculate more (as opposed to invest), and do a poorer job of selecting stocks that will appreciate. Overconfident investors take more risk than average; this may be because they don't diversify properly or because they gravitate to riskier stocks. Is this you? Margin can have its place, but it shouldn't be a consistent part of your investment strategy. The market offers a healthy return over time and margin often forces investors—or to be more precise, your broker might force you—to make the wrong decision at the wrong time. Investors who don't use margin have the luxury of staying invested and even buying more in the midst of a bear market. Which investor would you rather be? Margined and at the mercy of your broker who is forcing you to reduce your risk because stocks are down and you've exhausted the limits of your margin account? Or unmargined and ready to take advantage? Regardless, we tend to be more overconfident when we have a strong desire for a particular outcome—say, building a successful retirement portfolio—because it's on us now.

Of all of the behavioral quirks and biases, the tendency to be overly confident may be the most dangerous. Humans tend to be more overconfident when a task is difficult or complex. There is probably no human undertaking more complex than constructing and operating a nuclear power plant, yet we manage to be overconfident even then.

Japan is one of the most earthquake-prone places on earth. Despite that, it is also one of the most reliant on nuclear power for electricity generation. Or at least it was until 2:46 p.m. on March 11, 2011, when a 9.0 magnitude earthquake struck in the Pacific Ocean, eighty miles east of the city of Sendai.

The Fukushima Daiichi nuclear power plant is located sixty miles south of Sendai on a rocky outcropping overlooking the ocean. It includes six reactors and is one of the largest nuclear power plants in the world. All nuclear power plants in Japan are built on bedrock because it is supposed to resist ground acceleration which is the side-to-side shaking that causes structural damage during an earthquake. Nonetheless, the Sendai earthquake resulted in three of the six Daiichi reactors exceeding their maximum horizontal acceleration design limits. Knowing that earthquakes can generate tsunamis, the reactors were built about thirty-three feet above sea level because an analysis of a tsunami that occurred in Chile in 1960 left designers confident that anything more than ten feet above sea level would be safe. (This requirement was raised to nineteen feet in 2002.) The tsunami that struck Fukushima on March 11 was more than forty-nine feet tall.

The reactors themselves survived the earthquake but all six external power lines to the reactor complex were destroyed, leaving Fukushima ironically reliant on emergency diesel generators to power its safety equipment. Those generators were located in the basements of the buildings that housed the turbines which turned superheated steam into electricity. When the first tsunami struck forty-one minutes later, followed by the second eight minutes after that, seawater poured into the basements. The diesel generators and all the electrical gear, which was also located in the basements of the turbine buildings, were flooded. There was now no external power to the plant and no internal emergency power available to one of the largest nuclear power plants in the world. That meant there was no way to keep the nuclear cores cooled. Core damage began in Reactor 1 four hours later. It began in Reactors 2 and 3 within seventy-seven hours. Shortly after the damage to the core commenced, the amount of radioactive cesium in the ocean near the plants was fifty million times higher than normal. Fukushima will never generate electricity again and it will take decades to clean up the radioactive mess.

Designers of Fukushima Daiichi were overconfident about nearly every aspect of how an earthquake might impact their nuclear power plant. They even managed to dismiss a report by the US Nuclear Regulatory Commission warning that a loss of power and failed backup diesel generators due to an earthquake was one of the "most likely" external causes of a nuclear accident.

The construction of any nuclear power plant is fraught and should compel designers to ask themselves millions of questions. Are our estimates correct? Can the buildings withstand the horizontal forces? What if there is a tsunami more powerful than the one in Chile? Maybe those questions and millions of others were asked and answered, but it seems that the mode was one of overconfidence in the ability to understand the worst-case scenario and then build something that would survive it. It was as if the designers had never heard of Murphy's Law. If all of Japan can be overconfident about something as potentially dangerous as nuclear power, then every investor has to guard against overconfidence with their portfolio. Do you tend to say something can't happen in the market? You're being overconfident.

AVAILABILITY BIAS

Availability bias is the tendency to use the most easily recalled events to estimate the probability of something occurring rather than using a truer analysis of historical likelihoods or base rates. When trying to estimate the likelihood of something happening, we think back to how often it has occurred in the past. Naturally, the most vivid occurrences come to mind first and crowd out all the times when nothing happened. For example, Americans overestimate the likelihood of dying in a plane crash because crashes tend to be gruesome and newsworthy. But from 2010 to 2017, there were zero passenger deaths in the United States as a result of accidents involving scheduled commercial air service. During the same period, 275,662 Americans died in automobile accidents but those don't stand out. Do you fall for this? Can you start asking yourself if you're thinking of the most striking examples of something (an airplane crash) or the most common examples of something (a fatal automobile accident)? Just asking yourself this question is a good start.

Recency is related to availability. While the most dramatic occurrences tend to come to mind, the most recent come to mind as well. This is why people who have recently had a friend go through a divorce tend to overestimate the frequency of divorce in the general population. That's also why basing investment decisions on what has happened recently, even if it's a massive downdraft in the Dow, is the wrong approach. We've already mentioned those overconfident investors who believe that the improbable, such as a stock market crash, is impossible and that the likely, such as a moderate annual gain in the broad market, is certain.

At the other end of the spectrum are investors who allow availability bias to sway them into thinking that the most extreme outcome is far more likely than it is. These investors behave as if a crash is always around the corner—and some of them are extremely sophisticated option traders. Professor Oleg Bondarenko pointed out in a research study that important parts of the US index option market are consistently priced in a way that suggests a crash of the magnitude of Black Monday in October 1987 will occur about every sixteen months. We've discussed how investors tend to construct portfolios as if they'll use the money in about one year, even if they don't intend to use the money for decades, and while they don't seem to believe that a crash is right around the corner, that self-imposed and inappropriate time frame means that some of them take less risk, and generate lower returns, than they reasonably should.

Why do investors do this? Because the average investor

may have no idea what happens in the stock market on an average day but nearly every single one can at least describe what happened in 2008 or 2000 or 1987 or 1929.

The tool to overcome this tendency is to understand what is normal rather than what is dramatic and easily called to mind. We've seen what is normal in the stock market for time frames from one day to a decade. Your job as an investor is to remember that the normal is more important to success than the dramatic.

LOSS AVERSION

Loss aversion is the very human tendency to dislike losses to a greater degree than we like gains. Loss aversion is logical when a relatively large loss makes us more sensitive to similar, subsequent losses because a subsequent loss would consume an even greater proportion of our net worth. But loss aversion is illogical when it prevents us from making an advantageous bet like the one that would pay us $200 if we called a coin flip correctly but cost us just $100 if we got it wrong. This tendency sometimes keeps investors with even long time frames from investing or from investing a reasonably large percentage of their portfolio in stocks even though, historically, they generate a return that more than compensates for the additional risk. When researchers quantify the effect experimentally, they find that losses hurt about twice as intensely as gains feel good. Add the fact that the Dow has historically lost ground on 47 percent of all trading days, and that average daily losses tend to be slightly larger than average daily gains, and it becomes easy to understand. Do you fall for this? Do you forget that losses are part of investing but that the odds are on your side over a long enough time line? Do you forget that if you're consistently putting money into the stock market—say, through monthly 401(k) contributions—then you probably *want* the stock market to be cheaper now.

The tool to account for loss aversion is to remember that you're not investing for a single day and the odds of the stock market generating a positive return improve as the time frame gets longer. We've learned just how much the odds improve as the investing time frame changes, but remember, there's no reason for loss aversion to keep anyone out of the stock market if they have a reasonably long horizon.

Even if a "bettor" requires a $200 payout to accept the possibility of a $100 loss, the US stock market has historically offered that ratio if the holding period is at least three years. For all three-year periods since the launch of the Dow, if the period shows a gain, the average return is 37.1 percent. If the Dow lost ground during the period, the average loss is 17.9 percent. As we've discussed previously, this doesn't include dividends which would make this ratio still more attractive but even without dividends, the three-year loss-aversion ratio of 2.07 should be sufficient for most investors. The five-year time frame shows a loss-aversion ratio of more than 3 (average gain of 59.1 percent versus average loss of 19.6 percent), which should satisfy all but the most loss averse. The ten-year time frame should absolutely satisfy everyone because it shows a loss-aversion ratio of 6.4 (average gain of 107.2 percent and an average loss of 16.7 percent).

But too often an investor's mental holding period is much shorter than their actual one. That leads to avoiding or underweighting stocks in a portfolio and that hurts returns. Fear is understandable, and it sometimes serves us well, but when it becomes the most important emotion while we're in the midst of constructing or maintaining a portfolio, it is not so helpful.

It's not just fear of financial losses that lead to illogical financial choices. Any fear can diminish a person's willingness to assume financial risks. In a study of financial risk taking, four economists exposed test subjects who were financial professionals to random electrical shocks while they were engaged in an investment task. All participants faced both high and low fear trials. A high fear level would be established by telling the participant they would receive painful, random electric shocks during the next three testing trials while a low fear level would be established in other instances by explaining they would receive shocks but these would be "mild and painless." When the test subjects were facing the fear of receiving a painful shock, they were not willing to assume as much financial risk. The researchers point out that it is not the actual shock but the anticipatory fear that affected risk taking.

Few Americans experienced more financial fear than the ones who lived through the 1929 stock market crash and Great Depression. The Dow fell for four consecutive years beginning with 1929, and lost 89.2 percent from the high made in September of that year to the low it made in July 1932. If you'd invested $1 in the Dow on May 26, 1896 and left it untouched for the next thirty-six years, on the day the stock market index sank to its lowest point in July 1932 you'd have gained about three-quarters of one cent. Employment dropped by twenty million with one in four Americans out of work. Fear was rampant but it was also persistent, and you've certainly heard stories about it. If you're old enough, you may even have heard stories from your grandparents. Americans who lived through the Great Depression were less willing to take financial risk even decades later. If they did take any risk, they were less likely to bear the risk of owning stocks and if they did own stock it made up a smaller portion of their portfolio. The same ends up being true for individuals who have experienced lower stock market returns during other periods—such as the early 1970s when the Dow fell by more than 40 percent in a grinding bear market that some thought would never end. This is one reason Americans were underinvested in the stock market when it finally took off in the early 1980s.

The Great Depression is the example investors use when they want to counter the idea that you're going to invest and stay invested and that's understandable. Only the overconfident would say a stock market crash of that magnitude is impossible. It *is* possible. But it is incredibly unlikely. The sort of investing on margin that fueled the bubble of the 1920s has been scaled back dramatically. The US Securities and Exchange Commission was created in 1934 to wring the most abusive tactics from our stock market and it has largely succeeded. Finally, the Federal Reserve understands how to respond to a stock market crash—something that wasn't true in 1929 when it actually made things worse. The Fed isn't perfect but it is substantially better at responding to crises than it was in 1929.

Again, only the overconfident would say the 1930s can't happen again but considering how our stock market has matured since the 1890s, when panics and crashes were common, through 1907, 1929, 1987, 2000, 2007, and 2020, the much greater risk is not being invested during a crash, but not investing *enough* the rest of the time.

Fear, including the fear encapsulated in loss aversion, has a logical component. But you're going to stay invested in a sensibly diversified portfolio and you're not going to be like the bettors at the racetrack when the horses are lining up for the last race of the day and lose your mind by trying to get back to even all at once. Investing works in the long-term; it doesn't have to work in the short-term too.

HERDING BIAS

When investors are fearful or uncertain, they will tend to herd, meaning they follow and mimic what they see and hear other investors doing. Unfortunately, investors also herd when they're confident. It's rarely optimal for them. Do you feel more confident if an investment thesis is shared by others? Isn't it possible that means the stock has already been bid up by those others? And would you trust those others in any other arena? Often the answer is no, but we'll tag along at the tail end of the stock-buying herd because it makes us more comfortable.

Many believe that our tendency to herd is evolutionary in that those who stuck together were less likely to become a predator's dinner. But it's also true that merely being part of a group changes your world and the way you see it. The test subjects who changed their answers in the test that involved assessing three-dimensional shapes did so in order to go along with the herd because the preparations for the test—introducing the subjects to each other, having them participate in friendly practice rounds, and displaying their vote next to their name and photo—changed their world. This may be the most obvious example of how merely being part of a group, or a herd, changes our approach to the world; it isn't helpful, but there's a reason for it. If the cost and time required to process information and come to our own conclusions become higher than normal then the incentive to herd is increased. Think back to high school and ask yourself if there were times when you went along with the crowd only because you weren't mature enough to come to your own conclusion. Then ask yourself if you sometimes get swept up by the stock market in the same way.

Some investors attempt to dress up herding as a legitimate investment strategy by calling it "momentum investing"—is if they were borrowing from physics and Newton's immutable laws of motion. As we've seen, there's no such thing as momentum in markets; the market is no more likely to rise tomorrow simply because it went up today.

As investors herd, they tend to buy the same stocks. After all, herding entails looking around and mimicking what others are doing. The result is certain meme stocks or sectors that are priced well above any fundamental estimate of their future value merely because the person next to you has bought it. For millions of Americans who would not trust a restaurant recommendation from the person standing next to them, following along with their stock purchases seems silly.

Beyond buying what everyone else has bought already, and after they have already bid up the price, herding limits the number of rational reactions to those we see other herd members choosing. When the original herding turns out to be a mistake, as it often does, investors are left with fewer ways to respond. Herding in the stock market is painful on the way up because the herd has overpaid; it is painful on the way down because responses are limited. We'd like to think that as Americans, investors are strong-willed individuals who forge their own path. Too often, as herding demonstrates, we're still more like high school kids.

John Maynard Keynes pointed out that, to a certain degree, all investing is about herding. That's because many investors are not trying to pick the best companies but are instead trying to pick the companies that the herd thinks are best. If the herd thinks XYZ Corp. is the best company, whether it is or not, then it will buy its shares and the price will increase. If ABC Corp. is actually the best company—meaning the most profitable with the best long-term prospects—but nobody knows about it, then its stock price won't move much until it reports great earnings, impressing some investors enough to buy its shares. If the herd still doesn't know about it then it won't move much until the next great earnings report. The good company will appreciate slowly and over a long period while the company beloved by the herd will appreciate rapidly until price outpaces value by a wide enough margin that the price falls back. This is why legendary investor Warren Buffett says that in the short term, the stock market is a voting machine [with the herd stuffing the ballot box], and over the long term it is a weighing machine, meaning the real value will be discovered. The differences between the two approaches, voting and weighing, or price and value, can be extreme. It can also be maddening because where do you stop once the question is no longer "What will everyone else pick?" but becomes "What does everyone else think everyone else will pick?"

Keynes's introduction to herding may have been a contest that was popular in British newspapers in the 1930s. Beauty contests grew into a familiar advertising gimmick as it became more economical for newspapers to publish photos. Originally, the winner would be picked by a panel of judges. Then some marketer realized that engaging readers would make the whole exercise more memorable. Readers were asked to pick not the six prettiest faces, but instead the six faces that they thought would correspond most closely to the other readers' choices. As Keynes wrote, "We have reached the third degree [of the problem] where we devote our intelligences to anticipating what average opinion expects the average opinion to be."

While this exercise ends up twisting back on itself when applied to the stock market, it also wastes investors' time which we already know is a scarce resource. But some feel compelled to do it because the divergence between real value (the most attractive face or most valuable company) and the average opinion of real value (what most people think most people think is the most attractive face) can be substantial.

To quantify this, National Public Radio ran an updated version of the "beauty contest" experiment. Twelve thousand people participated and each was presented with photos of three animals. The first was a kitten, the second was a baby polar bear, and the third was a slow loris, an odd-looking primate with a smallish head and oversized eyes. Half the participants were asked to select the animal they personally found the cutest. The other half was asked to select the animal they thought most participants would think was cutest. It was as if the first half were being asked to pick the best stock while the second half was being asked to pick the stock they thought other market participants thought was best.

Half the participants selected the kitten as the cutest animal, 27 percent picked the slow loris, and 23 percent chose the baby polar bear. We can consider these percentages the actual measures of value. But in the other version of the test, the one that asked participants what they thought others would pick, the kitten received 76 percent of the votes, the slow loris received 15 percent, and the baby polar bear, just 10 percent. (The results don't sum to 100 percent due to rounding.) We can consider these the market prices. When trying to outguess the group, the price for the kitten was half-again too high while the prices for the slow loris and baby polar bear were about half of what they should have been. The herd is not very good at aligning value and price.

How can investors fight against herding behavior considering that going against the herd is emotionally draining and can be genuinely uncomfortable? Habits are powerful because they don't require much thinking. To the degree that you can put your investing on auto pilot you will avoid herding. By staying away from nichey investments or meme stocks and instead focusing on broad-based products, you'll largely avoid the herd.

It is certainly true that the herd can take entire markets to levels they don't deserve, as it did with the stock market in the 1920s, 1980s, and 1999. Herding can take other asset classes to levels they don't deserve, as it did with tulip bulbs in the 1630s, gold and silver in 1980, and the housing market in the first half of the aughts. But you can avoid the hottest, shiniest stocks or sectors and make out better in the long run.

A little introspection is also helpful here. Why are you buying? Why are you buying now? Why can't you wait thirty days? Answers to these questions, particularly if they're accompanied by impatience, can suggest a mistake is in the making. Once again, go easy on yourself because herding is natural. It may be fundamental to who we are and how we used to survive, but herding is no longer a defense against those who would like to feed off of you. It is instead playing into the hands of those investors who aren't herding and are instead selling what you're buying or buying what you're selling. It has been said that the stock market is a mechanism for moving wealth from the impatient to the patient. Don't be impatient.

OVERREACTION

It always feels like the right reaction at the time, yet rarely is. Investors overreact to the recent and the dramatic. They overreact to the short term and ephemeral and trade billions of shares of stock, even on days when there is no fundamental news. They overreact during crashes and panics and the stocks that are hurt the most end up doing best during the subsequent recovery. They overreact over longer time frames, as Professors De Bondt and Thaler showed by assembling portfolios of the best performers and worst performers and demonstrating that the

Loser portfolio later outperforms the Winner portfolio if both the formation period and holding period are reasonably long. Investors overreact to news, particularly bad news, in nearly every way and across every time frame imaginable. Ask yourself how you react to surprising news. Is your tendency to believe that action is more likely to be appropriate than inaction? This is an important bias that you may not recognize.

Some psychologists say we overreact because overreaction used to have very little cost in an environment when underreacting could have serious consequences. That sort of evolutionary imprinting is difficult to turn off, even if it ends up being wrong and frequently expensive. It is also illogical, as anyone who has gotten incandescently angry after being cut off in traffic would likely agree after cooling down a bit.

One common way in which investors overreact to crashes and bear markets is to stop investing entirely. They stop making contributions to investment accounts because they don't want to deal with the regret of buying today and seeing a loss next month. (Loss aversion at work!) We saw the proof of this in chapter 3, when we detailed that during roaring bull markets investors put even more money into traditional equity mutual funds (0.23 percent of existing assets each month) than they did during all months (0.20 percent of existing assets per month), and that when times are bad, they really step on the brakes (inflows of just 0.01 percent of existing assets per month). Investors stop buying almost completely when Wall Street is in a bear market. Is this you? The time to ask yourself is when the market is relatively calm. The time to remind yourself of your answer is when it is anything but. The idea that investors would rather pay higher prices during a rally and stop buying when prices are lower should be the first clue that we overreact and that it is illogical.

Another way in which investors overreact is to sell the bottom. Those same equity mutual fund investors pulled assets out of the stock market during six of the twelve months in 2009. They took out the most in March, the month the market fell to its lowest level. They withdrew the second-highest amount in February. In other words, they sold at the worst possible time and it was due to overreaction and overreliance on the most recent, most dramatic news. Is this you? If you've done this in the past, ask yourself why you fell for this bias. Write down your thoughts. Put it someplace you can find it when the market is falling. Reread it and assimilate your own lesson.

The same pattern of overreaction existed in 1987. Investors added to equity mutual funds in every one of the first nine months of the year as the Dow rallied by 13.8 percent in January, more than 3 percent in both February and March, and more than 5 percent in both June and July. It was up 43.6 percent for the year before the end of August. Investors waited as the market gave back all it had gained, then they overreacted and pulled money out in October, November, and December, but only after the market was below where it had started the year. This included a net withdrawal of more than 4 percent of assets in October, the month of the crash, in what was the biggest monthly net withdrawal since the 1950s. In the first half of the year the salient returns, the recent returns, hadn't been normal but investors bought. The return during October was particularly salient but it wasn't normal either, yet investors sold.

A Checklist for Better Investing

Although overreaction hurts returns, individual investors can take some comfort in knowing that it's common; even professional traders and analysts overreact. Professor De Bondt described the forecasted changes predicted by professional stock market analysts as "too extreme to be considered rational." As he and his colleague Richard Thaler found in another paper, there is considerable evidence that the forecasts of professional analysts "display the same overreaction bias" as those of "naïve undergraduates." There's even data which demonstrates that professional foreign exchange traders overreact when predicting moves for foreign currencies and that economists overreact when predicting changes in macroeconomic variables such as inflation, industrial production, housing starts, and retail sales.

Simply put, investors tend to overreact. This means they buy into bubbles and sell into crashes and bear markets. You don't have to join them. We're not all in the market together.

This is where "Do no harm" comes in. Since investors of all stripes tend to overreact, maybe the better reaction is no reaction at all. You'll continue to make regular contributions to savings and retirement accounts, so by not reacting we mean no gratuitous trading like those who get carried away. If that means not making additional purchases beyond your regular investment regime in the midst of a bubble, then congratulations. If it means not selling at the bottom like all those mutual fund investors in October 1987 or in February and March 2009, then congratulations. It may feel like you're supposed to be doing *something*, but often, almost always, the best thing for your portfolio is to do nothing other than stay on course.

THE SOCIAL DYNAMIC OF INVESTING

Nothing disproves the notion that every investor is rational all the time more completely than the fact that investing is largely a social activity. Herding occurs because of the social aspect of investing in that we see and discuss what others are doing so we do it too, even when we suspect they're wrong. One cause of the disposition effect is our desire to tell others about our winners or avoid having to tell them about our losers. Availability bias skews our appreciation of risk because of the things we hear about, and the things we hear about socially are often the most salient, meaning they're the most impactful.

Professor Shiller is more emphatic. In a paper he published in 1984, he wrote, "Investing in speculative assets is a social activity. Investors spend a substantial part of their leisure time discussing investments, reading about investments, or gossiping about others' successes or failures in investing." Does this impact how you actually deploy money? Answering this is an important step in understanding yourself and improving your investment performance.

To the degree that social interaction leads an investor to hear about a stock or fund they didn't know about, or leads to learning about new techniques, then it is a wonderful thing. But think about your recent social interactions regarding investing and ask yourself if they educate or merely entertain. Unfortunately, our social interactions in the investing realm are rarely truly productive.

As Shiller goes on to point out, "It is thus plausible that investors' behavior (and hence prices of speculative assets) would be influenced by social movements. Attitudes or fashions seem to fluctuate in many other popular topics of conversation, such as food, clothing, health, or politics. These fluctuations in attitude often occur widely in the population and often appear without any apparent logical reason. It is plausible that attitudes or fashions regarding investments would also change spontaneously or in arbitrary social reaction to some widely noted events." In other words, believing that we're fully rational and completely analytical when money is involved is crazy.

Shiller wrote about investing as fashion in 1984 but he wasn't the only one equating the two during that decade. In 1987 Robert Prechter was a force on Wall Street. He had graduated from Yale in 1971 with a degree in psychology and initially spent four years as a drummer in a rock band. In 1975, he decided to put his psychology training to work in the stock market and took a job with Merrill Lynch.

After turning his attention to investing, Prechter came across an obscure but grandly named book, *Nature's Law—The Secret of the Universe*, published in 1946 by Ralph Nelson Elliott, a disabled former accountant from Marysville, Kansas. Elliott hypothesized that the stock market moves in fractal waves across a range of time frames. Prechter became a disciple of Elliott's approach and grew to believe that not only does the stock market move in waves, but that the waves are driven by broad social trends as the national mood swings between optimism and pessimism.

By 1979, Prechter was working for himself, publishing an investing newsletter based on his wave theories. He first came to prominence after he heard the British punk band the Sex Pistols and thought their apocalyptic lyrics, such as "No future, no future, no future," "I am an Antichrist," and "Anarchy in the UK" marked a low point in the national mood that would also be a low point for the US stock market. Prechter was right, at least about the direction for the stock market.

Prechter continued to ride his waves and became a celebrity in his own right. In May 1987 he was profiled in *People* magazine and introduced mainstream investors to his theories that mood impacts how we invest. He told investors that the season's shorter skirts were a "clear rising trend" for the market and suggested they buy. When asked if investors would be better off reading *Women's Wear Daily* than the *Wall Street Journal*, Prechter responded, "Exactly." Prechter would turn bearish later and his vocal warning in early October was one spark for that month's crash.

It is easy to dismiss the idea that the unintelligible lyrics of a British punk-rock band or the length of skirts can give insight into the direction of the stock market. It seems unserious and farfetched. But Professor Shiller would go on to receive the Nobel Prize in Economics for his approach to asset pricing and there's nothing unserious about that. We're human; nearly everything we do has a social aspect. That includes fashion, sports, politics, and investing. But ask yourself if the social dynamic changes how you invest or what you invest in. If the answer to either is yes, then the social dynamic is likely to be harming your investment returns.

PHANTASTIC OBJECTS

The stock market doesn't know what investments you own, nor does it care. The charismatic founders of those fascinating companies that make computers and phones and electric cars don't know what you own and they don't care either. And buying those things is not going to make you more interesting or attractive any more than buying a certain pair of basketball shoes will help you sink three-pointers like your childhood hero.

But this is a consideration for investors because everyone wants to be psychologically transported somewhere else if it means getting away from our workaday world, even if it's just for the length of a daydream. Some investors start getting drawn in, thinking that a new company or technology is going to change the world and that they'd like to be along for the ride. The real trouble begins when those investors start to believe that whatever it is that makes a company special will rub off on them. Do you do that? Do you think that whatever it is that seems to make a handful of companies special right now will make you a little more special if you own their shares? When that happens, investors should examine the process that got them to this point, because there was a time in the past when RCA (founded in 1919 as Radio Corporation of America) seemed like a magical company. It was defunct and sold for scrap in 1986. The stories told about Xerox, Sears, and Kodak are similar. Phantastic companies become also-rans and some are lucky to survive at all. Remind yourself of this if you own Tesla or Apple or Google for any reason other than the profits it will earn and pass along to shareholders.

Professors David Tuckett and Richard Taffler are the ones responsible for the idea of phantastic objects and how internet stocks and the founders of those companies became objects of fascination and desire, leading some investors to become transported. They point out that this occurs in a "predictable emotional direction" and that the process unfolds in stages. The first is some intermittent excitement about a new product or innovation. That is followed by a growing sense of excitement, then mania or euphoria, and then an apex is reached, after which the process moves through panic and finally blame.

It's normal for an investor who is curious about the world to find new products and companies that are fascinating. You may even believe that a company's founder is a unique talent who is building a product that is going to lead to a fundamental change in our lives while making a tremendous amount of money for shareholders. That sounds like a wonderful investment thesis and an investor might get excited about the prospect. But when excitement moves to mania or euphoria, like it did with internet stocks in the 1990s, that same curious investor should wonder about his reaction and be careful about letting himself get pulled into a process that is no longer about investment success but is instead about the emotional catharsis that comes from phantastic objects. Is this you?

AFFECT

Affect is more familiar to most people as mood but there's an important distinction. Mood seems to impact our actions in both directions; happy leads to certain responses and sad leads to different responses. Affect is a phenomenon that stokes fear, an emotion we don't just experience but also feel. Unfortunately, affect doesn't work in the other direction.

Since affect works on the level of feelings, you may not even be aware of its influence. That means it can be easier for you to rely on the feelings driven by affect than on an objective evaluation of probability-weighted outcomes. Several researchers have shown that feelings become a more important element in decision-making as complexity and uncertainty increase, as they do during a stock market crash. Do you tend to lean into a task as the complexity and uncertainty increase, or are you more like most of us, with the tendency to back away? Knowing this about yourself will help you understand how affect is likely to impact your investment decisions. It is the rare individual who prefers ambiguity and complexity. It is the rare market that doesn't offer ambiguity and complexity in enormous servings.

We've already discussed how judgments regarding risk tend to occur in an emotional context; this is why an accurate self-assessment is important. We know how we're likely to feel if risk works against us, just as Paul Samuelson's colleague knew how he'd feel if he lost their wager, but again, that's after the fact.

Affect's most powerful impact occurs before we make the decision to take a risk, and it often determines whether we take the risk at all. Investors are often primed with negative affect or mood thanks to the availability bias. You'll remember how reading about a student who died of leukemia led test subjects to increase their subjective estimates of the likelihood of dying in entirely unrelated ways, including due to an airplane crash or lightning strike. Something similar occurs with investors. The availability bias leads sophisticated index option traders to increase their subjective probability of the likelihood of a stock market crash and a segment of the index option market is regularly priced in a way that suggests stock market crashes occur several times each decade. But availability and affect lead even normal investors to think that stock market crashes occur about ten times more frequently than they do. Because their beliefs are wrong, they tend to make poor decisions in the way they invest.

Good investors don't overtrade and they don't have to devote hours and hours to managing their portfolios. But they do have to pay attention to their affect, their mood, when they sit down to allocate money or rebalance their portfolio. If judgments regarding risk are not emotionally neutral, then a little emotional self-awareness is helpful.

ANCHORING

Imagine you are searching for a new house and you find one you like. It is offered for sale at $600,000. What is your next step? Do you offer $540,000, which would be a 10 percent discount from the asking price? Do you offer $570,000, which would be a 5 percent discount? Do you offer some other amount?

While some readers are asking themselves how much money they're going to shave off the asking price by negotiating, others are asking a different question: How much is the house *worth*? This exercise is an example of anchoring. When you read $600,000, that became an anchor and for some readers their next step relied on that number even though they have no way of knowing if it is relevant. It may not be as irrelevant as the randomly selected number in Kahneman and Tversky's test that asked about the percentage of United Nations countries that are in Africa, but, as in that test, the asking price is only a starting point in the search for the actual value. Be honest, did you come up with some number you would offer the sellers or did you ignore the anchor and ask yourself what the house is worth? Both are fine—in fact, it's probably most instructive if some number came to mind—but you have to remember that you have this tendency and account for it when investing.

Anchoring is the mental bias that relies *inappropriately* on the first, available, or most recent information when making a decision. For many investors, the anchor price for a stock in their portfolio is the price they paid. While that anchor fades with time as other prices are more recent and become more available, for many stocks, the price you paid becomes even more important than the price it's trading at right now.

Anchoring is related to the disposition effect because the purchase price is the anchor price; many investors see their activity change fundamentally around this price. If the current price is above this anchor price (some researchers refer to it as the reference price), then the investor may very well sell the stock to lock in a profit and get that pleasurable jolt. If the current price is below this reference price, the investor is much less likely to sell and lock in a loss. The market doesn't know what you paid for the stock so why should your response be so completely different if the stock is at $102 and a $2-a-share winner as opposed to $98 and a $2-a-share loser?

Anchor pricing keeps investors from selling losers, not because it suggests the price is going to go up in the future but merely because it's dropped in the past. Like many of the biases, anchoring means that investors focus not on what a stock is likely to do in the future but rather on what it has already done. That's like driving by looking in the rearview mirror rather than through the windshield. Looking backward is a horrible way to manage your portfolio and doubly so if the only things you can see are the most memorable.

Over time, the purchase price will fade as the reference price for anchoring. What takes its place? Usually the new reference price is some combination of a recent price, the purchase price, and prices that are memorable for whatever reason, but the speed with which investors update or change their reference price depends on whether the stock has rallied or dropped since they purchased it. Investors tend to update their reference point more quickly if the stock has rallied than if it has dropped. This is another echo of disposition. It is also a version of prospect theory as humans tend to be risk averse when they have a profit and risk seeking when they experience a loss.

The tool for overcoming anchoring is to forget your purchase price and remember that every stock is worth only what the market says it is in the moment. What you paid six months or two years ago is irrelevant other than for tax purposes. Then ask yourself where you think the stock will be in the future based on a time frame that makes sense for you and why you think it will be there. It's impossible to know, but if you have a solid fundamental response about other investors overreacting and selling the stock down because of a disappointing earnings report, then hang on. If your answer has to do with where the stock has been, you're not thinking productively.

FINANCIAL ATTENTION

We'd like to think that investors buy the best stocks. The truth is that they buy the stocks that grab their attention. Stocks can capture investors' attention by trading abnormally high volume or having a big percentage price move. They may captivate an investor only because they have a quirky founder or CEO who's good on social media. Another way in which a stock can seduce investors is to become well known for being famous, like some Hollywood celebrities. A group of stocks did that and they were known as the Nifty 50.

The Nifty 50 was a group of approximately fifty well-known stocks that attracted most of Wall Street's attention during the 1960s and early 70s. They were universally considered superlative investment candidates that were expected to grow in value, so investors herded in; often they were the only stocks a casual investor would hear about in an age before financial television.

All a company had to offer to be included was a compelling story and the potential for growth. There is no definitive list of the stocks in the Nifty 50—it wasn't an index per se—and the companies spanned a wide range of industries, from retailers to technology. There wasn't even a broad theme for the companies generally mentioned. Among the group, Xerox was a technology company but Avon sold cosmetics. Coca-Cola made soda but some of the members manufactured industrial chemicals or

beer. There were pharmaceutical companies, banks, and retailers. Xerox wasn't the only technology company because IBM
and Texas Instruments were members. But so was the Simplicity Pattern Company which made sewing patterns for the home
seamstress. The Nifty 50 stocks were written about in the financial pages and discussed whenever conversations turned to
investing. They were the stocks that got investors' attention.

That attention, and the ensuing buying pressure, made these
stocks extraordinarily expensive, often for no other reason than
because they were well known for being part of the Nifty 50.
Before Coca-Cola aired its magical "I'd like to buy the world
a Coke" commercial and before its disastrous experiment with
New Coke, it was part of the Nifty 50. Some investors thought
its sales would increase spectacularly and at the end of 1969 it
was trading at a price-to-earnings ratio of 36 meaning that its
share price was thirty-six times what the company was earning in
profit each year, per share. Its dividend yield, the amount of the
annual dividend divided by the stock price, was just 1.7 percent.
That's not very much when a ten-year Treasury note was yielding
7.9 percent, but Coke was well known so investors paid up.

Xerox was another member of the club, and understandably
so, as it was one of the leading technology companies of its time.
It introduced the first commercial copier in 1959 and the formerly sleepy maker of photographic paper became a sensation.
At the end of 1969 it was trading at a price-to-earnings ratio of
42. Its dividend yield was a nearly microscopic 0.8 percent.

Avon was more expensive than either of them with a P/E ratio
of 57. Its dividend yield? Just 1.2 percent. Avon had been founded
in 1886 by David McConnell, a door-to-door seller of books

who gave away makeup and perfume as gifts to female customers. Eventually he realized his customers were more interested in the beauty products than the books and he made the predictable change. McConnell hired his first female representative—what would later be known as the iconic Avon Lady—in 1896 when the company was still called the California Perfume Company. It was renamed Avon in the 1920s, inspired by the site of William Shakespeare's home. In 1969, the company's annual sales were nearing $1 billion and it was a darling of Wall Street, well known and expensive to investors because it had become famous.

The John Deere Company had been making farm implements for fifty years longer than any of these three had been around. It became the largest manufacturer of farm equipment and tractors in the United States in 1963 and was both immensely profitable and well ahead of its competition. It was also cheaper than Coke, Xerox, and Avon because it wasn't in the Nifty 50 so it didn't receive the same attention they did. John Deere's price-to-earnings ratio at the end of 1969 was 12 and its dividend yield was 5.3 percent. John Deere was two-thirds cheaper than Coke and cheaper still when compared with Xerox and Avon.

A company generally has a high price to earnings ratio because investors believe that it will increase its profits during the next few years and "grow" into the valuation Wall Street has bestowed. Occasionally that happens and the investor who paid a premium price feels vindicated. But paying a premium price doesn't leave much room for error and these stocks usually get pummeled during a bear market. Hopes for increasing profitability give way and investors who loved paying the high price that had been demanded become willing to sell for whatever they can get. It's often an overreaction to the downside but its genesis lies in the initial attention-driven overreaction to the upside.

The year 1970 was not a particularly good one for the stock market as the Dow gained just 4.8 percent. It was even worse for the expensive stocks in the Nifty 50. Coca-Cola gained just 3 percent. Avon did slightly better because it gained 3.2 percent. But Xerox lost 18.2 percent. The unloved John Deere remained unloved and lost 4.9 percent in 1970.

Then came the bear market of the early 1970s. The first Arab oil embargo in 1973–74 shattered America illusions of geo-political power in a region we had not paid much attention to prior to the start of the decade. Oil prices rose from $3 a barrel to $12 a barrel. A political scandal led to the first-ever resignation of a US president. From the end of 1969 to the end of 1974, the Dow lost 23 percent.

The most expensive stocks got marked down even more. From the end of 1969 to the end of 1974, Coke lost 35.6 percent. Xerox lost 51.3 percent and Avon lost 66.5 percent, nearly two-thirds of its value.

In this sort of broad-based downdraft, nearly every stock is going to lose ground but solid businesses that had been sell-ing at reasonable prices did better than the ones that were well known for being famous. From the end of 1969 to the end of 1974, John Deere gained 97.7 percent.

With so much financial media available now, it is natural for your attention to be drawn to certain stocks or funds. But then you have to ask yourself how you became aware of those you're considering investing in. Was it a disciplined search through all the available alternatives? Or was it the result of a conversation with a friend (a social interaction) or because you heard about it on TV or the internet because it made a big move or traded a bunch? Neither is a compelling reason to invest and the fact that the news was already out when it made its way to you is likely a reason to stay away. You're probably thinking this is an unfair conundrum: How do I uncover investment opportunities if I can't hear about them from friends or read about them, or come across them in the media? But ask yourself if the investment vehicles you hear about in these ways can really make up a core position in your portfolio or if they're an unimportant sideshow incapable of making a real difference in your investment return despite taking up much of your attention.

MYOPIC LOSS AVERSION

Myopic loss aversion is the result of a combination of factors. The first is the well-understood tendency for people to dislike losses more than they like profits. The second is the frequency with which investors look at their investing results and the subsequent tendency to focus too much attention on short-term outcomes rather than the time frame appropriate for the investor. A final factor is the tendency to look at each investment separately rather than reviewing the portfolio as a whole. Ask yourself if you're susceptible to any of these because all of this combines to hurt long-term performance.

Investors who evaluate their portfolio frequently tend to be more risk averse so they tend to have a smaller allocation to higher-risk equities and a larger allocation to lower-risk investments such as bonds or no-risk assets such as cash. There's nothing wrong with taking less risk than most investors if you're truly aligning the time frame expressed by your portfolio with the day you'll be using the money, but a one-year time horizon is not appropriate if you're investing your toddler's college fund. In many ways, the way to defeat myopic loss aversion is to set your portfolio and forget about it. Just let it compound and accumulate without evaluating it if the vagaries of the account balance might lead you to take less risk than is appropriate. Are you able to do this? If not, ask yourself why you're not able to do the thing that is appropriate, likely to result in better returns, and easier. Are you the person who can't wait for the water to boil? Are you the person who can't wait for your investments to compound without taking some action? Why?

Another reason some investors experience myopic loss aversion is the tendency to look at each component individually rather than as a holistic portfolio. Obsessing over a single loser, despite its being part of a portfolio that has done well, leads to illogical behavior and generally more risk aversion. Remember that the advantage of a portfolio is the diversification it offers and that the performance of a single component this week or this month is irrelevant. You're investing for the long term. Act like it.

OVERTRADING

Traditional economists would say that the amount of trading that occurs each day is simply illogical. During the decade of the 2000s, the average annual turnover of the stocks on the New York Stock Exchange was 180 percent meaning that, on average, every share of stock changed hands about once every seven months. In 2008, turnover was 282 percent with the average share of stock changing hands about once every four months. That's speculating, not investing. What are you, a speculator or investor? What should you be?

Even after markets returned to a more normal environment in the 2010s, trading occurred more frequently than a long-term investor could consider wise as turnover from 2013 through 2016 hovered at 160 percent.

Is there any legitimate reason for serious, long-term investors to turn over their portfolios twice a year? No. But it happens in the aggregate because some investors are actually gamblers seeking a thrill while others are overconfident that they know more than they do or that they'll be able to unravel the narrative because they think they saw it coming in the past. Trading is like many things; a little of it is good because you have to build a portfolio, occasionally make certain it is still properly diversified, and the like. Too much of it hurts returns because of trading commissions. And even for those who don't pay a commission, there's the cost of the bid-ask spread which can be substantial, particularly if it's paid many times a day for a large number of shares. Make no mistake, you are rarely going to buy the bid or sell the offer. Even if you put in a limit order, you're usually going to buy stock only when the market is willing to sell at that price, and you're going to sell stock only when the market is willing to buy at that price.

How much does overtrading hurt the average investor?

One study divided US households into quintiles based on their monthly turnover from 1991 to 1996. Each quintile contained about thirteen thousand households and the quintile that traded the most during that period earned an average annual return, net of trading costs including commissions, of 11.4 percent. The quintile that traded the least, and which could really be said to contain investors as opposed to speculators, gained 18.5 percent. Less trading generated an additional 7.1 percentage points each year. By the way, the average annual return for the S&P during that period, including dividends, was 18.4 percent. These real investors beat the index slightly; the traders trailed substantially. Which would you rather be? Which are you?

It is difficult to know if we're going to be particularly susceptible to many of the behavioral biases that appear when money is concerned. Disposition is a function of your brain chemistry and as addiction studies prove, we're all different in that regard. Some may give in to affect and be more impacted by moods than others. But it's easier to know who will overtrade. It tends to be men, particularly single men, because they tend to be the most overconfident. That confidence is misplaced.

The tool here is to not trade any more than necessary to implement your diversification plan. Yes, a tiny bit of additional trading helps defeat information overload and that's beneficial during the worst times so go ahead and trade, but ask yourself why. Ask if it's for the thrill of it or in pursuit of sensation. Then ask yourself again. It's okay to admit this is the reason. In fact, it is commendable to admit that is the reason. But if it is, then go watch a horror movie or find the nearest roller coaster instead.

We'll treat investing as a social event, paying more attention to what our neighbor says or to whatever stands out in the news rather than to what we learn on our own. The result will be owning the shiniest stocks rather than the best stocks, leaving us under-diversified in a world where that makes sense only in the context of how supremely suboptimal our biases can make our decisions.

The key is to ask yourself how you became aware of the opportunity and look at its base rate of return. Then tell yourself that you will revisit the opportunity in a month and mark that date on your calendar. At that point, you can reexamine the potential investment but not because of its current salience; it will no longer be the shiny new object. And since we're trying to invest rather than trade, the thirty-day waiting period should have little impact on your long-term returns. In fact, it will likely end up having a positive effect when you recognize what was going on in your head thirty days before and move on to something else.

And if you still can't bring yourself to do these things, then realize it might be time to hire a professional to manage your investments. Nobody ever said you can't do that but they're not immune to biases either.

THE ANXIOUS INVESTOR CHECKLIST

We've looked at some of the important behavioral biases in a new way here, devoid of the specific historical context that can separate them from our individual experience. But ask yourself if you fall for them. Ask how you get investment ideas, how you evaluate them, how and why you execute them, and how you manage them once they're part of your portfolio. Nobody is going to judge, so be honest. Then be proud of yourself for the improvement and personal growth. You've already become a better investor just by examining how and why you act.

Investing is a noble endeavor. You're deferring gratification today to provide for a better future for yourself and others. But you are also the biggest barrier to investing successfully. This is a condition that can be remedied by introspection and thought. Get to it.

In the 1940s, Americans, including the ones who bought war bonds at Younkers Brothers Department store in Des Moines, were anxious over the course of the World War II. You may be nervous now if the stock market seems to be coming apart and taking your retirement or kid's college fund with it. Your imagining is almost certain to be worse than reality. Some thought they would never recover financially following the Great Recession of 2008–09. But those who didn't overextend themselves to buy a home or were impervious to the biases came out fine, if a little unsettled by the whole episode. Remember that because that is the lesson the anxious investor should learn. Be logical beforehand, stalwart during, and you'll be successful afterward.

You realize just how many people helped, and how much you relied on them, when you sit down to thank everyone who made your work possible.

A profound thank-you to Nick Amphlett at HarperCollins for the initial nugget of an idea for this book. He understood how rich the topic would end up being and how much fun it would be to write about.

Another profound thank-you to David Fugate at Launch Books for helping this book see the light of day. Without him it never would have. David is a wonderful sounding board and provider of the needed reality check.

Thank you to Joseph Davis who was a wonderful resource in tracking down prices of a number of defunct and delisted stocks. You'd think finding stock prices for some of the internet bubbles biggest failures would be relatively easy. I know it is not, even if Joseph makes it look like it is.

Thank you to Michelle Mwangi for her assistance in finding additional data.

I appreciate all the help from the smart people at Hawthorne Strategy Group, as they were gracious in providing creative and marketing support.

Writing this book required reading a substantial number of academic papers and I'm constantly amazed that so many accomplished and busy professors are happy to respond to questions and requests for guidance. Their willingness to help someone who is a novice in their specific field is very much appreciated. Those who were particularly generous include:

Professor Terrance Odean of The University of California–Berkeley is one of the world's experts on overconfidence among investors and he was a wonderful and gracious resource. His academic papers also have the benefit of being eminently readable.

Professor David Tuckett of University College London, along with his research partner Richard Taffler, has done fascinating work on the impact of phantastic relationships on our view of the financial world and selection of the investments we make. Professor Tuckett was very generous in helping me understand the psychological issues that are subconsciously at work as investors get transported by novel products and iconoclastic founders.

Professor Andrew Odlyzko of the University of Minnesota is the world's leading expert on Isaac Newton's misadventures in the South Sea Company bubble and he was very helpful in correcting my errors and misunderstandings. Some of the contemporaneous materials are tough to find or difficult to read

Acknowledgments

and Professor Odlyzko was incredibly considerate in finding or deciphering them.

Thank you to Professor Mike Cooper of the University of Utah for sharing his list of companies that changed their names to take advantage of the internet bubble. His paper "A Rose. com by Any Other Name" (written with Orlin Dimitrov and P. Raghavendra Rau) is a fascinating insight to the craziness surrounding the dot-com bubble.

Thank you to Saqib Ahmed of Reuters in tracking down some of the most obscure stock prices, including ones for the fancifully named New York Bagel Exchange.

Thank you to the Investment Company Institute for mutual fund flow data.

Finally, thank you to everyone who read chapters and offered feedback. Pat and Mike Cafferata have been dear friends for decades and they were the first who agreed to dive in. They were tremendous help.

Keith Colestock has also been a friend forever and Keith is also an extremely accomplished investment professional. Keith offered important thoughts that would have escaped anyone else.

Mark Abssy is another financial professional who provided important insight and didn't hesitate to point out when I was veering from the important point into minutiae.

Bill Maher, Dennis DuPont, and Rob Leonard all offered comments and thoughts that were helpful. Bill, in particular, pointed out when something wasn't working and gave me the courage to delete finished pages that had taken weeks of work because they just weren't helpful. Dennis and Rob were also essential and all were willing to spend too much of a week talking about this book when we were supposed to be just hiking and playing golf.

A dozen other people were willing to provide their time, and I appreciate it.

And of course, thanks to Wendi for putting up with me, even when the writing wasn't going well. She's the best possible partner and I'm incredibly lucky.

Any errors are mine and mine alone.

Closing levels for the Dow Jones Industrial Average and S&P 500 index are from S&P/Dow Jones. Closing levels for Nasdaq indexes are from Nasdaq, Inc. Most prices for individual stocks, particularly for defunct stocks, are from the Center for Research in Security Prices (CRSP) at the University of Chicago. Data for other asset classes comes from a variety of sources, including Yale University. Macroeconomic data including unemployment data and the Fed Funds rate are generally from the St. Louis Federal Reserves's FRED database.

So much has been written about what we call the Great Recession that an author has an embarrassment of riches. Less has been written about the internet bubble and even less about the South Sea Company bubble but there is plenty about each of them for the interested reader.

PREFACE

The story of Younkers Department Store and its role in World War II bond drives is told in "First the War, Then the Future:

Younkers Department Store and the Projection of a Civic Image during World War II" which appeared in *The Annals of Iowa*, volume 73, Winter 2014.

The estimate for the cost of World War II comes from the Congressional Research Service, "Costs of Major U.S. Wars" by Stephen Daggett, Specialist in Defense Policy and Budgets, June 29, 2010.

SOUTH SEA BUBBLE

Isaac Newton has been the subject of several biographies and much is known about his life even if the questions about his name continue among a small circle of researchers. One such biography is *Never Rest, A Biography of Isaac Newton* by Richard Westfall. It contains a number of contemporaneous images of Isaac.

Much has been written about the South Sea Company bubble. One of the first to describe it was Charles Mackay in his seminal *Memoirs of Extraordinary Popular Delusions and The Madness of Crowds*, which was published in 1841. Famed economist John Kenneth Galbraith also wrote about it in his work *A Short History of Financial Euphoria*. Dale, Johnson, and Tang wrote more specifically about the subscription schemes in "Financial Markets Can Go Mad: Evidence of Irrational Behavior During the South Sea Bubble," which appeared in the *Economic History Review*, LVIII, 2, (2005), pp. 233–271. The British National Archives also has a substantial amount of information regarding the bubble. Professor Andrew Odlyzko is the final word in all aspects of the subscription agreements and Isaac Newton's participation. He's written extensively about both and shared his insights and understanding of the specifics, including the *Flying Post* article, with the author via email. Historical prices for South Sea shares came from a variety of sources including the Yale School of Management, International Center for Finance, South Sea Bubble 1720 Project.

The Old Testament mention of distributing land according to a random drawing is found in Numbers, 26:55. The history of lottery loans and other lotteries as a means of raising capital for the public weal is discussed in "Lottery Loans in the Eighteenth Century" by Francois R. Velde, the Federal Reserve Bank of Chicago, February 1, 2017.

While the term "animal spirits" had been used previously in other contexts, one of its first uses in the context of economics was by John Maynard Keynes in his 1936 book, *The General Theory of Employment, Interest, and Money*.

Much has been written about sensation seeking among investors. The papers which address this phenomenon among hedge fund managers include "Sensation-Seeking Hedge Funds" by Brown, Lu, Ray, and Teo from September 2018. The paper that analyzes Finnish drivers is titled "Sensation Seeking, Overconfidence, and Trading Activity" by Grinblatt and Keloharju from March 2009. Both were published in *The Journal of Finance*.

The story of lotteries in Taiwan is told in the *Handbook of the Economics of Finance*, chapter 22, "The Behavior of Individual Investors" by Barber and Odean and in *Taiwan Review*, "Lotto Fever," May 1, 2002.

The quote from Keynes regarding "gambling instinct" is in his work *The General Theory of Employment, Interest, and Money* in the chapter "The State of Long-Term Expectation."

Information regarding London's public coffee houses as financial centers in 1720 comes from a variety of sources including "Coffee Houses, the Press and Misinformation," Princeton University Press, which is the source of the quote regarding "most companies trading in joynt-stocks."

The story of the South Sea bubble is told ably in *Devil Take the Hindmost—A History of Financial Speculation* by Edward Chancellor, and he describes details of the subscription campaigns on page 67. Andrew Odlyzko provides the definitive details of Newton's activity in a variety of publications including "Newton's Financial Misadventures in the South Sea Bubble," which was published on November 13, 2017, as well as "Isaac Newton and the Perils of the Financial South Sea," which appeared in *Physics Today*, July 1, 2020.

Information regarding the disposition effect including brain activity can be found at "The Role of the Striatum in Social Behavior" by Baez-Mendoza and Schultz published in *Frontiers in Neuroscience*, December 10, 2013. Details regarding the lack of a pleasurable spike in brain chemistry if an investor avoids the disposition effect can be found in "The Psychology and Neuroscience of Financial Decision Making" by Frydman and Camerer, which appeared in *Trends in Cognitive Sciences*, September 2016, pp. 661–675. The other study mentioned is "Learning by Trading" by Seru, Shumway, and Stoffman. The study of professional fund managers can be found in "How the Disposition Effect and Momentum Impact Investment

Professionals," which appeared in *The Journal of Investment Consulting*, Volume 8, Number 2, summer 2007. Information regarding investors succumbing to the disposition effect in down markets and the impact it has during subsequent recoveries is available in "The Disposition Effect in Boom and Bust Markets" by Barnard, Loos, and Weber, which was published in February 2021. A discussion of the social aspect of the disposition effect, including the idea that being part of a social network nearly doubles the magnitude of the effect, is found in "Peer Pressure: Social Interaction and the Disposition Effect" by Rawley Heimer of the Federal Reserve Bank of Cleveland.

The study that quantifies the returns of the winners sold versus the losers kept is described in "Are Investors Reluctant to Realize Their Losses" by Terrance Odean, December 1997. Details of the performance of Japanese investors during their bull market from 1984 to 1989 is found in "The Behavior of Japanese Individual Investors During Bull and Bear Markets" by Kim and Nofsinger.

Details for the various South Sea Company subscription schemes are found in "Financial Markets Can Go Mad: Evidence of Irrational Behavior During the South Sea Bubble" by Dale, Johnson, and Tang, 2005, and also from Odlyzko

The quotes regarding the popularity of the South Sea Company as a topic of conversation come from a variety of sources including Harvard University Library's exhibition "The South Sea Bubble, 1720."

The "Bubble Companies" that were launched to take advantage of the South Sea Company mania are discussed in detail in Carswell's *The South Sea Bubble*, in Mackay's *Memoirs*, and in Chancellor's *Devil Take the Hindmost*. Odlyzko discusses the most egregious in "An Undertaking of Great Advantage, But Nobody to Know What It Is—Bubbles and Gullibility" in *Financial History*, Winter 2020. The quote regarding "credulous investors" is found in "An Historical and Chronological Deduction of the Origin of Commerce," Volume III.

The specifics of Newton's purchases and sales of South Sea shares are found in "Isaac Newton and the Perils of the Financial South Sea" by Odlyzko. The fact that the total market capitalization of the South Sea Company was five times the total GDP of Great Britain is from Odlyzko in an email to the author.

Overconfidence among humans has been studied extensively and it is also a rich subject in the context of trading and investing. One of the first, and most striking, academic studies of overconfidence is the one that describes how so many of us believe we are above-average drivers. That study is "Are We All Less Risky and More Skillful Than Our Fellow Drivers" by Ola Svenson from 1981. One study that focuses on overconfidence as we age is "The Development of the Illusion of Control and Sense of Agency in 7- to 12-Year-Old Children and Adults" by van Elk, Rutjens, and van der Pligt from 2015.

Odean's paper "Do Investors Trade Too Much" describes the sort of overconfidence that leads to overtrading.

The conclusion that meteorologists and handicappers at racetracks are some of the professionals who find their confidence and their actual ability to be in sync, or "well calibrated," comes from "Aspects of Investor Psychology" by Kahneman and Riepe.

The paper that describes Professor Robert Shiller's survey of investors immediately following the 1987 crash is "Investor Behavior in the October 1987 Stock Market Crash: Survey Evidence" and was published by the National Bureau of Economic Research (NBER) as their working paper No. 2446.

Some of the first evidence of the difference between females and males regarding overconfidence and respective approach to investing is "Boys Will Be Boys: Gender, Overconfidence, and Common Stock Investment" by Barber and Odean, *The Quarterly Journal of Economics*, February 2001.

Research regarding the amount of risk taken by investors who have recently lost money comes from "Investor Behavior and Economic Cycles" by Beryl Chang.

The striking research regarding overconfidence in those answering questions on a test of general knowledge and how those who are absolutely certain they got the answer correct yet are wrong 16.9 percent of the time, is from "Knowing with Certainty: The Appropriateness of Extreme Confidence" by Fischoff, Slovic, and Lichtenstein in 1977.

The story of AIG and its enormous losses from credit default swaps has been told several times, including by the author in his previous book, *A History of the United States in Five Crashes*.

Shiller's survey regarding "contagion of interest" including social interaction is "Survey Evidence on Diffusion of Interest Among Institutional Investors" by Shiller and Pound, March 1986.

The story of Paul Samuelson's proposed coin flip bet and how it was rejected is told in "Risk and Uncertainty: A Fallacy of Large Numbers" by Paul Samuelson, 1963.

Many have researched prospect theory and loss aversion. The initial paper regarding prospect theory is by Kahneman and Tversky, "Prospect Theory: An Analysis of Decision Under Risk" which appeared in *Econometrica* in March 1979.

The shift from loss aversion to risk seeking has been the subject of substantial research. Professor Richard Thaler discusses it in chapter 30 of his book *Misbehaving*. Details regarding how bettors at racetracks bet too much on longshots and how they become more risk-seeking at the end of the day is told in "Probability and Utility Estimates for Racetrack Bettors" by Mukhtar Ali in the *Journal of Political Economy* as well as in "Who Buys Lottery Stocks" by Larry Swedroe and in "An Examination of the Empirical Derivatives of the Favorite-Longshot Bias in Racetrack Betting" by Sobel and Raines.

The quotes regarding the panic as South Sea shares collapsed come from Applebee's *Original Weekly Journal*, October 1, 1720.

Notes regarding regret, including that it is stronger for decisions that result in action then for decision that don't generate action, come from "Investor Psychology and Asset Pricing" by David Hirschler, page 12. The idea that some litigants will choose to settle in order to avoid regret rather than merely reduce or eliminate risk is from "Better Settle Than Sorry: The Regret Aversion Theory of Litigation Behavior" by Chris Guthrie, Associate Professor Law, University of Missouri.

An interesting analysis of status quo bias is found in "Status Quo Bias in Decision Making" by Samuelson and Zeckhauser, 1988. The story of the "New Coke" debacle is told on the Coca-Cola Company's website, www.Coca-ColaCompany.com, under the Company History tab.

Information regarding the correlation between the weather in New York City and returns for the stocks listed on the New York Stock Exchange can be found at "Good Day Sunshine: Stock Returns and the Weather" by Hirschliefer and Shumway, 2003. Data regarding sales of lottery tickets in Ohio in the days following a victory by the Ohio State University football team can be found in "The Role of Potential Loss in the Influence of Affect on Risk-Taking Behavior" by Arkes, Herren, and Isen.

DOT-COM BUBBLE

While some has been written about the South Sea bubble, that is dwarfed by what has been written about the internet bubble and collapse. One general work that is worthwhile is *dot.con, How America Lost Its Mind and Money in the Internet Era* by John Cassidy.

Details of the NEI Webworld scam are included in several *Los Angeles Times* articles including one by Walter Hamilton that appeared on December 16, 1999. CNN also covered the scam and its fallout. The story of how indictments for the Webworld pump-and-dump were "good" news for the stock can be found in the *Wall Street Journal*, December 17, 1999, as reported by Rebecca Buckman.

The story of the creation of the internet has been told many times. The role Tim Berners-Lee played is described by the World Wide Web Foundation at https://webfoundation.org/about/vision/history-of-the-web/. Development of the Mosaic web browser, Marc Andreessen's move to Silicon Valley, and the creation of Netscape is told by Cassidy and in Jim Clark's autobiography, *Netscape Time*. The *New York Times* story extoling the virtues of the first browsers appeared on December 8, 1993. Information regarding Yahoo, AOL, eBay, and other early web-based businesses is found in various sources including eBay's own website.

John D. Rockefeller and Standard Oil are covered by Ron Chernow in his book *Titan: The Life of John D. Rockefeller, Sr.*

The concept of phantastic (sic) stocks and how investors are "transported," is explained in papers coauthored by professors David Tuckett and Richard Taffler. Those papers include: "Phantastic Objects and the Financial Market's Sense of Reality: A Psychoanalytic Contribution to the Understanding of Stock Market Instability" which was published in the *International Journal of Psychoanalysis* in 2008, and "A Psychoanalytic Interpretation of Dot.com Stock Valuations" which was published in March 2005. This second work is the one which specifically says "investors became caught up emotionally with the [internet bubble] drama." Professor Tuckett was also generous in sharing his insight with the author via email. The concept of transportation is specifically discussed in "The Role of Transportation in the Persuasiveness of Public Narratives" by Melanie C. Green and Timothy C. Brock, which was published in the *Journal of Personality and Social Psychology*, 2000, Vol. 79, No. 5, pp. 701–721.

Information regarding the word "mindshare" is from the Google Ngram of "Mindshare" as of May 2021. The quote regarding valuation not being a helpful tool is from a *New York Times* interview of Henry Blodget regarding Internet Capital

Group. The story was written by Gretchen Morgenson and appeared on March 18, 2001.

Details regarding AOL's acquisition of Netscape in November 1998 are available from a variety of media outlets including Bloomberg, the *Wall Street Journal*, and CNN.

Information regarding early internet companies is available from many outlets. Information regarding the agreement between Kozmo.com and Starbucks was included in a story describing the transaction in the *Wall Street Journal* on February 14, 2000 which was written by George Anders. The quote from the Kozmo executive regarding retailing through the internet is from the documentary movie *E-Dreams*, at 1:09:31.

Details about Pets.com are widely available, including in a Bloomberg article dated March 5, 2000, by Arlene Weintraub. Information regarding the sock puppet mascot is available from *AdWeek*, December 11, 2000. Superbowl commercials for nascent dot-com companies which ultimately failed are available to view on YouTube.

The phenomena of recency bias is explained in a number of papers including "The Behavior of Individual Investors," which appears in the *Handbook of the Economics of Finance*, chapter 22. The literature regarding "Home Bias" and the tendency for investors to inappropriately invest in companies in the industry in which they are employed, or in companies headquartered near their home, is summarized by Hersh Shefrin on page 26 in "Behavioralizing Finance" which appeared in *Foundations and Trends in Finance*, Vol. 4, Nos. 1–2, 2009.

Availability bias is discussed in "Availability: A Heuristic for Judging Frequency and Probability" by Amos Tversky and

Daniel Kahneman which appeared in *Cognitive Psychology*, 1973, 4, pp. 207–232.

Cause of death data is from the Centers for Disease Control.

Affect is discussed in a number of academic papers including "Affect, Media and Earthquakes: Determinants of Crash Beliefs from Investor Surveys" by Goetzmann, Kim, and Shiller, which was published December 8, 2017, as well as "Affect, Generalization, and the Perception of Risk" by Johnson and Tversky, 1983. Risk as feelings is examined in "Risk as Feelings" by Loewenstein, Hsee, Weber, and Welch, which appeared in the *Psychological Bulletin*, 2001, Vol. 127, No. 2, pp. 267–286.

The story of the Palm Pilot and 3Com's spinoff of Palm is told in the *New York Times*, September 14, 1999, and the *Wall Street Journal*, March 3, 2000.

ComputerLiteracy.com's name change is described by the *Wall Street Journal* in an article titled "Overhaul" by Peter Loftus, which appeared on November 22, 1999. Price data for New York Bagel Exchange is from Refinitiv via their Datastream service. Information regarding the broader trend in dot-com–related name changes is from "A Rose.Com by Any Other Name" from Cooper, Dimitrov, and Rau, September 17, 2000.

Details regarding second-tier IPOs during the last days of the internet bubble are from a variety of sources including the *Wall Street Journal* and the *New York Times*.

Information regarding adoption of the internet and AOL's market share is from Pew Research and www.NTIA.doc.gov.

Data quantifying revenue and earnings for Amazon and Yahoo come from those company's annual reports.

Judge Jackson's ruling that Microsoft had abused its monopoly power is available on the U.S. Justice Department website. Other information regarding the case is available from the *New York Times*, *Wired Magazine*, CNET.com, and Bloomberg.

A number of biases are described in "Judgement under Uncertainty: Heuristics and Biases" by Tversky and Kahneman which appeared in the journal *Science*, New Series, Vol. 185, No. 4157, on September 27, 1974. Anchoring and the question regarding the percentage of countries in the United Nations that are from Africa is discussed on page 1,128. Contemporary data regarding the proportion of UN nations from Africa is from the United Nations website, UN.org.

Tversky and Kahneman's seminal paper describing Prospect Theory is "Prospect Theory: An Analysis of Decision Under Risk" and it first appeared in *Econometrica*, Volume 47, Number 2, March 1979.

The story of internet-related name changes made to avoid being associated with the internet bust is told in "Managerial Actions in Response to a Market Downturn: Valuation Effects of Name Changes in the dot.com Decline" by Cooper, Khorana, Osobov, Patel, and Rau. Professor Cooper was the source of the list of companies cited in the two studies.

THE GREAT RECESSION

Details for the Lehman Brothers bankruptcy filing are available from a number of outlets including the *Wall Street Journal*, MarketWatch, and CNN. Some details are from the actual filing, which is: U.S. Bankruptcy Court, Southern District of New York, Bankruptcy Petition #: 08-13555-scc.

Information regarding the G.I. Bill can be found at Defense .gov. Details of the history of the U.S. mortgage market and homeownership can be found in *A History of the United States in Five Crashes* by the author. They can also be found at huduser.gov and in the St. Louis Federal Reserve's FRED database.

Housing prices cited are based on the S&P CoreLogic Case/Shiller Home Price Indices. Details regarding the size of the mortgage-backed security market, HSBC, New Century Financial, Bear Stearns, and other topics come from a variety of sources including a *Wall Street Journal* article dated February 8, 2007 by Carrick Mollenkamp, a *New York Times* article dated April 2, 2007, CNN, and another *Wall Street Journal* Article dated July 17, 2007.

The story of bundled and tranched mortgages has been told several times including in *A History of the United States in Five Crashes*. Growth in the size of the mortgage-backed securities market is available from Statista.com and the World Bank.

Details of the Bear Stearns hedge funds, Merrill Lynch's involvement, and the funds' collapse has been told in the financial press including in the *Wall Street Journal*. Information regarding Merrill Lynch comes from a variety of sources including the company and the *New York Times*, October 30, 2007. The article regarding Countrywide Financial seeing trouble ahead is from the *Wall Street Journal*, July 25, 2007. The story of Bear Stearns's co-president's note to clients and subsequent resignation is told in the *Wall Street Journal*, August 6, 2007.

Source Notes

Information regarding the litany of bad news in September and October 2007 comes from a variety of sources including the *Wall Street Journal*, the Wharton School, and the St. Louis Federal Reserve. Information regarding Goldman Sachs and the amount of "Level 3" assets it owned is from Sec.gov, the company, and the *Wall Street Journal*, October 10, 2007. The story regarding the percentage of securities that are traded in arms-length transactions on exchanges appeared in the *Wall Street Journal*, October 12, 2007 and was written by Susan Pulliam, Randall Smith, and Michael Siconolfi.

Citigroup's overconfidence regarding the safety of its mortgage-backed security holdings is told in a *New York Times* article that appeared on November 22, 2008, and was reported by Eric Dash and Julie Creswell. The story of Northern Rock's failure is told in several outlets including BBC.com. AIG's potential involvement in a rescue of Northern Rock is told by the BBC and *Wall Street Journal* in an article published October 13, 2007. Other details regarding the failure of AIG, including some of the obscene quotes regarding the depth of their trouble, come from a variety of sources including *All the Devils Are Here* by Bethany McLean and Joe Nocera. Details regarding AIG's reckless selling of credit default swaps and general inanity are provided in a number of outlets including "What Went Wrong at AIG" published by Northwestern University's Kellogg School of Management.

Information regarding financial attention and the "Ostrich Effect" can be found in academic papers including "The Ostrich Effect: Selective Attention to Information" by Karlsson,

Loewenstein, and Seppi, published in 2009, and "Financial Attention" by Sicherman, Loewenstein, Seppi, and Utkus, published in 2015. Information regarding attention's impact on individual investors' stock selection is detailed in "All That Glitters: The Effect of Attention and News on the Buying Behavior of Individual and Institutional Investors" by Barber and Odean, 2007. The paper regarding advertising and investor engagement is titled "Advertising, Breadth of Ownership, and Liquidity" by Grullon, Kanatas, and Weston, April 2004. Details of the impact of the timing of earnings announcements and investor attention are included in the *Handbook of the Economics of Finance*, chapter 22, "The Behavior of Individual Investors" by Barber and Odean, page 1559.

Morgan Stanley's results data is courtesy of the company. Information regarding Merrill Lynch's results, write-down, and capital raising efforts at the end of 2007 and beginning of 2008 are told in the *New York Times* including in articles dated December 25, 2007; January 2, 2008; January 15, 2008; January 17, 2008; and January 18, 2008. The sad story of Springfield, Massachusetts's misadventure in mortgage-backed securities is told in the *Wall Street Journal*, January 21, 2008.

The story of herding as it occurred among thieves at the Petrified Forest National Park is told in "Crafting Normative Messages to Protect the Environment," which appeared in *Current Directions in Psychological Science* by Robert B. Cialdini, 2003, and "The Science Behind Why People Follow the Crowd," which appeared in *Psychology Today*, May 24, 2017, and from the National Park Service website, NPS.gov. Herding among Korean investors during the 1997–1998 Asian economic crisis is described in "Foreign Portfolio Investors Before and During a Crisis," NBER No. 6968, p. 9 and table 4. Herding among those who think they are part of a group who are evaluating three-dimensional shapes is described in "Neurobiological Correlates of Social Conformity and Independence During Mental Rotation" by Berns, Chappelow, Zink, Pagnoni, Martin-Skurski, and Richards, 2005.

The fascinating tendency for starlings to "herd" is told in "What Is a Starling Murmuration and Why Do They Form" by the Wildlife Trust for Lancashire, Manchester, and North Merseyside. Hypnotic video is available on NPR.org and other outlets.

The internal debate regarding AIG's write-down is told in *A History of the United States in Five Crashes.* Fed Chair Ben Bernanke's warning about bank failures was reported in the *Wall Street Journal* on March 1, 2008. Details from spring 2008 come from a variety of sources including the *Wall Street Journal*, *New York Times*, and others.

Several academic papers have studied information overload in a number of settings. One of the best in the context of investing is "Asset Allocation and Information Overload: The Influence of Information Display, Asset Choice, and Investor Experience" by Agnew and Szykman, May 2004.

The history of Lehman Brothers is told by several outlets including the Corporate Finance Institute. Merrill Lynch's profligate spending in the summer of 2008 is told by CNBC.com and the *Wall Street Journal*. The June 19, 2008, criminal crackdown on mortgage bankers and real estate developers is discussed in Wharton's timeline of the Great Recession.

Fannie Mae and its history, along with that of the other GSEs, is told in a variety of outlets including Huduser.gov, CNN, the *Wall Street Journal*, and *On the Brink* by Henry M. Paulson, Jr. who was Secretary of the Treasury at the time.

The story of Lehman Brothers's bankruptcy filing and Bank of America's acquisition of Merrill Lynch has been told in many outlets including the *New York Times*, *Wall Street Journal*, *Too Big To Fail* by Andrew Ross Sorkin, and *On the Brink*.

Thomas Bayes's work and use of this theorem is discussed in many outlets. One excellent source is *The Theory That Would Not Die* by Sharon Bertsch McGrayne.

Kahneman and Tversky's paper regarding overreaction is titled "Intuitive Prediction: Biases and Corrective Procedures" and was published in June 1977. Data regarding overreaction to stock splits is from "The Market Reaction to Stock Splits" by Lamoureaux and Poon and from "Volatility Increases Subsequent to Stock Splits: An Empirical Aberration" by Ohlson and Penman. Keynes's quote is from his seminal work *The General Theory of Employment, Interest, and Money*, page 138.

Mutual fund flow data is from the Investment Company Institute. ETF flow data is from Morningstar's "Morningstar Fund Flows and Investment Trends, Annual Report 2009."

The academic study regarding investor's ignorance regarding their past performance is "Why Inexperienced Investors Do Not Learn: They Do Not Know Their Past Portfolio Performance" by Glaser and Weber, 2007. The study of Finnish investors and the disposition effect is "Learning by Trading" by Seru, Shumway, and Stoffman which appeared in the *Review of Financial Studies*.

The number of Americans who lost their homes to fore-closure during the Great Recession is from the *Los Angeles Times*, September 15, 2018.

CHAPTER 4

Data for the Dow Jones Industrial Average and S&P 500 come from S&P Dow Jones Indices. Data for treasury notes comes from Yale University. Housing price data uses the S&P Core-Logic Case-Shiller National Home Price Index. Calculation of returns and correlations are from the author.

The Benartzi and Thaler paper is "Myopic Loss Aversion and the Equity Premium Puzzle," May 1993, NBER Working Paper No. 4369. Their conclusion that investors focus on one-year returns appears on page 5.

Status quo bias is examined in "Status Quo Bias in Decision Making" by William Samuelson and Richard Zeckhauser, which appeared in the *Journal of Risk and Uncertainty*, Vol. 1, No. 1 (March 1988), pp. 7–59.

Disposition effect is described in "The Disposition to Sell Winners Too Early and Ride Losers Too Long: Theory and Evidence" by Shefrin and Statman, 1985. Professor Odean's paper is "Are Investors Reluctant to Realize Their Losses?" which was published in December 1997.

Overreaction and De Bondt and Thaler's "Winner" and "Loser" portfolios are described in "Does the Stock Market Overreact?" which appeared in *The Journal of Finance*, Vol. XL, No. 3, July 1985.

One excellent analysis of hindsight bias in finance was done in the paper "Hindsight Bias, Risk Perception, and Investment Performance" by Biais and Weber which appeared in *Management Science*, Vol. 55, No. 6, June 2009, pp. 1018–1029.

Overconfidence has been studied extensively, including in the domain of investing and finance. One good example is "Leverage Overconfidence" by Barber, Huang, Ko, and Odean which was published in 2019. It describes the kaleidoscope of ways in which overconfidence leads to poor investment practices and inferior returns.

Details regarding the earthquake and tsunami that destroyed the Fukushima-Daiichi nuclear power plant are from the U.S. Geological Survey at usgs.gov and from other sources. Information regarding the nuclear reactors comes from the World Nuclear Association at World-Nuclear.org. Data regarding radiation in the ocean is from Woods Hole Oceanographic Institution at whoi.edu.

Data regarding deaths from commercial air travel and automobile accidents comes from Airlines for America at Airlines.org and the Insurance Institute for Highway Safety at iihs.org respectively.

The paper that describes availability bias in certain domestic index option markets is "Why Are Put Options So Expensive" by Oleg Bondarenko, which was published in November 2003.

Loss aversion is related to prospect theory and the foundational work in prospect theory appears in Kahneman and Tversky's *Econometrica* paper mentioned earlier. Even earlier work in loss aversion was done by Harry Markowitz, who received the Nobel Prize in economics in 1990. Markowitz's paper is "The Utility of Wealth" and was published in 1952.

A tremendous amount of research into herding has been undertaken. Some is detailed in "Herd Behavior in Financial Markets: A Review" by Bikhchandani and Sharma, which is in the IMF Working Paper published in March 2000. The paper that details herding among Korean investors is "Foreign Portfolio Investors Before and During a Crisis" by Kim and Wei in NBER Working Paper No. 6968. Keynes observation that we are now "anticipating what average opinion expects the average opinion to be" appears in his *General Theory of Employment, Interest, and Money* on page 156. NPR's modern version of the beauty contest is detailed on NPR.org in an article titled "Our Cute Animal Experiment, Explained" which was published on January 11, 2011.

Most of the details regarding overreaction come from "Does the Stock Market Overreact" by De Bondt and Thaler and "Do Security Analysts Overreact?" which is also by De Bondt and Thaler.

The social aspect of investing is a relatively new topic for research but Shiller's 1984 paper is "Stock Prices and Social Dynamics" 1984, p. 457. Information regarding Robert Prechter is from Elliottwave.com and the *Chicago Tribune*, October 23, 1987.

Information regarding "Phantastic Objects" is available in the papers by Tuckett and Taffler previously cited.

Affect's impact on investors is explained in "Affect, Media, and Earthquakes: Determinants of Crash Beliefs From Investor Surveys" by Goetzman, Kim, and Shiller, 2017.

The classic research into anchoring is presented in "Judgement Under Uncertainty: Heuristics and Biases" by Tversky and Kahneman, which appeared in *Science* magazine, No. 185, pp. 1124–1131. Another interesting paper is "Reference-Point Formation and Updating" by Baucells, Weber, and Welfens, which was published in 2011.

Much has been written in the mainstream media about the Nifty 50 stocks from the 1960s. This Nifty 50 should not be confused with the Nifty 50 benchmark of Indian stocks listed on India's National Stock Exchange. Our Nifty 50 is discussed extensively in *Forbes* magazine and by Professors Jeff Fesenmaier and Gary Smith of Pomona College. Stock prices in the discussion of the Nifty 50 are from the Center for Research in Security Prices at the University of Chicago. PE data is from Wharton Research Data Services.

Myopic loss aversion is introduced in the paper "Myopic Loss Aversion and the Equity Premium Puzzle" by Shlomo Benartzi and Richard Thaler, which was published as NBER Working Paper No. 4369 in May 1993. Other important papers include "Can Myopic Loss Aversion Explain the Equity Premium Puzzle? Evidence from a Natural Field Experiment with Professional Traders" by Larson, List, and Metcalfe from September 2016 and "The Effect of Myopia and Loss Aversion on Risk Taking: An Experimental Test" by Thaler, Tversky, Kahneman and Schwartz, which was published in May 1997 in *The Quarterly Journal of Economics*.

Trading data including annual turnover on the New York Stock Exchange comes from the St. Louis Federal Reverse's FRED database. Details of the study that quantifies the harm done by overtrading can be found in "The Behavior of Individual Investors" which is chapter 22 of the *Handbook of the Economics of Finance*. It was written by Barber and Odean in 2013 and the details appear on page 1540.

The paper that Ben Bernanke wrote about mistakes made by the Federal Reserve during the 1930s is titled "Nonmonetary Effects of the Financial Crisis in the Propagation of the Great Depression," which appeared in *The American Economic Review*, Vol. 73, No. 3, June 1983.

Index

Index